My desire went on burning Me. It vanquished them and they shall be nothing. The LORD shall be lame. He shall be made a stranger- Jesus my Messiah.

See p. 42 for explanation of the above matrix

(Scientific Breakthrough Validates the Divine origin of The Bible)

Glenn David Bauscher

Lulu Publishing

Divine Contact-Discovery of The Original New Testament
(Scientific Breakthrough Validates the Divine origin of The Bible)
by Glenn David Bauscher

Lulu Publishing

ISBN:978-0-6151-5604-0

Table of Contents

Preface & Dedicatory

Your attention ,please ! What I have written in this book demands a preliminary explanation and advertisement, not for the book's sake, but for a discovery which I believe is probably too mind boggling for most to easily accept.

What I believe I have found is the original New Testament as it was originally penned by the apostles, without any errors whatsoever. That would be an outrageous enough claim in itself, and I am making it here. But I am going far beyond that. I claim, and present scientific evidence to demonstrate, verified by scientific experiments, that God Himself is the Author behind that New Testament , which He wrote letter for letter ,in the Aramaic language, by the hands of the human apostles of Jesus of Nazareth, Who is The Christ.

Divine Contact-The Original New Testament Discovered

Imagine that hidden in an edition of Shakespeare's complete works in English was found the following , by skipping **99,021** letters, 67 times, starting at the first letter -"W" -in Hamlet, Act 1, scene one: **"William Shakespeare will become the most famous English playwright in the world."** Would you believe Shakespeare had put the 68 letter code there himself deliberately ? How could he have done so ? The code would stretch through 6.3 million letters of text, covering all his works more than twice, connected from end to beginning ! He would have had to compose each work in the order starting with **Hamlet** in the middle of the volume, then the play after it in the book, etc, to the end of the book, then he would have had to compose the first play in the book, after the last play in the book, and then the next, until we come again to Hamlet, which would have to have been written after itself and after the book written after it, and so on and so forth ! Another alternative is that Shakespeare had written all 1252 pages of his plays at one sitting and insured that the code , with **99,021** letters between each code letter , as long a text as **Hamlet** ,longer than **Julius Caesar** & most of his plays , was precisely spaced and went through the entire text of the 1904 Oxford University Press edition, two times, end to beginning!

Then six other similar codes were found in Shakespeare, of similar length , some even longer, with skip lengths even longer in some, and going around the whole volume up to a dozen times for one code. Some of the codes were found to read backwards, starting at the middle of the volume and working toward the beginning, then continuing at the end and going around several times backwards to complete the code. Two involved long strings of letters that read one message forward and another backwards using exactly the same string of letters! These facts make it impossibly complicated for a human being to compose such codes that cycle around an entire book more than once . Each code , as its letters go through the same books a second time , magnifies the already extreme difficulty of its construction by geometric and large exponential proportions.How does one manage to write even one play with two code letters in it , each one spaced from a code letter in the plays before and after by 99,021 letters, and the same thing being repeated in the next play, and the next, and the next, through the entire 1252 pages and around the volume, like a cylinder, all fitting like a jigsaw puzzle of 3 million pieces, in which each piece must be counted twice in order for the puzzle to be assembled ?! Just for Shakespeare to count the letters between code letters each time, would have taken a month , assuming he counted two letters per second ! Simply to count from the first code letter to the second, 99,021 letters away, would have taken more than thirteen hours, at the counting rate of two letters per second ! How one keeps track of such numbers of letters as he is also composing and writing a play, is far beyond my imagination, and I have a pretty lively imagination.

But remember, he is juggling seven such codes in the same volume, each going through the same plays multiple times, each code letter separated by huge spaces of dozens of pages of text at a precise number of letters, each which he must count in order to construct that particular code. Neither can the number of letters in the text be altered by even one letter, or all of the existing code will disappear !

Just the counting of all the code letters for the seven codes would have taken about half a year, day and night (no sleep) at the generous rate of counting two letters per second, just once for each letter, without making one counting error, while writing his plays at the same time ! Let's give the poor man some sleep time of eight hours a day, and make that a year, counting twelve hours a day, so that he is not spending every waking moment counting ! That kind of counting would be a near impossibility in itself , aside from the coordination involved in writing and fitting the seven codes revolving around their orbits several times each, some forwards and some backwards, some both forwards and backwards ! The total picture of activities involved presents an impossibility multiplied by an impossibility, multiplied by an impossibility !

And did I mention that Shakespeare also wrote some codes in French ? In fact, some of the codes are in English and French, both at the same time ! The same letters can be spaced differently and read in French. Some read in English forward and in French backwards !

There are four or five possible explanations for the above :
1. Shakespeare did it intentionally. In that case, he would have to qualify as a superhuman intellect beyond anything ever imagined possible for a human.
2. It was sheer coincidence. The odds against that are beyond all odds verifying DNA or any other statistical proof.
3. An extraterrestrial dictated the text to Shakespeare or the editor at Oxford Univ. Press in 1904.
4. God dictated the text to Shakespeare and prearranged the book order for the Oxford Edition.
5. A time traveler from the future dictated the text to Shakespeare.

This above illustration is a reality, not in Shakespeare, but in The Peshitta New Testament in Aramaic. Only the names , languages and titles were changed were changed to protect the innocent. I have found seven such codes thus far; none is about Shakespeare, but each one is about Jesus The Christ (His birth , suffering , death or resurrection).

Even if The Peshitta were a translation, or any of the Aramaic NT books were translations, the text as it exits in the edition I have did not exist in any Peshitta scroll or codex in the fifth century or earlier. Many books exist in single book manuscripts or sections of the

Divine Contact-The Original New Testament Discovered

NT. Gospels are usually separate from Epistles. Western Peshitta mss. do not have Revelation or five of The General Epistles in the same text as the Critical edition in The Syriac NT.

No translator(s) could have pulled off a feat like what I have described, even with a super computer and super advanced software. I seriously doubt we will ever be able to invent such codes hidden in a text by spacing the letters so far apart , connecting the text end to beginning, and make several sentences or paragraphs in each one, all grammatically correct and coherent, each telling a related Gospel message about The Messiah, God and The Holy Spirit, The Birth, Suffering, Death and Resurrection of Yeshua Meshikha, each in beautiful **Aramaic** or **Hebrew** poetry !

 It appears to me that God put these codes in the Aramaic New Testament to be discovered in the computer age, when many are skeptical and without faith in God or The Bible, but have faith in technology. There were no computers when The New Testament was written, yet computer technology is required to find these codes I have found in The New Testament. *Since no mere human, reading or studying the text, could have found these codes without a computer, I affirm that no mere human in the first century or in any century before the computer age could have put them there*; nor would he have reason to. It would seem that the human difficulty of composing these codes would far exceed the difficulty of finding them. If the seven long codes are not proof enough, I have found millions of Divine Name codes in the NT, via an experiment, far beyond statistical chance occurrence numbers, that pinpoint The Codemaker's identity.

I further affirm that this discovery demonstrates at least eight truths:

1. The God and Christ of God of <u>The New Testament</u> exist and are exactly Who and What that New Testament says they are.
2. The New Testament in which these scientific proofs exist is absolutely true in all its statements, i.e.- **infallible**- historically, theologically, prophetically, scientifically, grammatically, geographically and textually-where it presents data concerning what pertains to the claimed statements and activities of God, Christ and The Holy Spirit. Whatever statements or actions are attributed to humans , angels or demons are also accurately recorded and are true history, though , unlike Divine statements, may not be necessarily true statements, since human and diabolical errors and lies are also accurately recorded.
3. The original New Testament was written in Aramaic and has been preserved to this day with 100% word accuracy in The 27 books of The Peshitta-Peshitto form I have tested, and in which I have found volumes of coded information.
4. Greek is not the original language in which any New Testament book was written.
5. The Greek New Testament is a translation of the original Aramaic text in all 27 books of the Western New Testament canon.
6. The number of letters in The original New Testament was and is **461,094**. It is possible that the completed text as written approx. 1950 years ago had some few spelling differences in a few places or compound word division differences, but the total number of letters was the same.
7. God and His Son love you eternally, and have provided for your eternal welfare and joy.
8. Nothing can separate you from that love.

The following is a sample of my translation of The Peshitta NT;It reads right to left:

61

(He answered him) עניהי (not) לא (& anything) ומדם (was) הוא (silent) שתיק (but) דין
הו (He)
(You) אנת (& he said) ואמר (Priest) כהנא (The High) רב (asked Him) שאלה (& again) ותוב
(of The Blessed One) דמברכא (The Son) ברה (The Messiah) משיחא (are ?) הו

62

(I AM *The Living God*) אנא אנא (to him) לה (said) אמר (Yeshua) ישוע (but) דין (he) הו
(Who sits) דיתב (of Man) דאנשא (The Son) לברה (& *you* shall behold) ותחזון
(of The Power) דחילא (the right *hand*) ימינא (at) מן
(of Heaven) שמיא (the clouds) ענני (on) על (& comes) ואתא

But He was silent and answered him nothing;and again The High Priest questioned Him and said,"Are You The Messiah, The Son of The Blessed One?" But Jesus said , "<u>I AM The Living God</u> , and you shall behold

Divine Contact-The Original New Testament Discovered

The Son of Man Who sits at the right hand of Power, and comes on the clouds of Heaven." (Bauscher's Aramaic-English Interlinear translation of The Peshitta Gospels) Mark 14:61,62

Read on, dear reader, read on . You are about to learn of what may be the most significant scientific and religious discovery since the resurrection of Jesus Christ !

(Proceed with caution; this is very intense and unusual material.)

Introduction:

I feel like a man who has just discovered a diamond mine and an oil field in his back yard ! This book is about a great discovery based on a scientific experiment , using the ancient Aramaic text of the New Testament-Aramaic is the language Jesus of Nazareth spoke. Mel Gibson is the first to widely publicize Aramaic in his powerful and world famous film, "The Passion of The Christ". This discovery has been several years in the making. I have analyzed thousands of experimental data and many thousands more data that confirm the discovery as real. I focused on mathematical analysis to verify the results statistically with the help of a professional mathematician and former fellow of the world's largest accounting firm – PriceWaterHouseCooper. He also finds the results convincing and more than highly significant.

What you are about to read in this book is a recent discovery and deals with a phenomenon which could change you. I believe it may change the world. Knowledge of Hebrew would be helpful but is not necessary to understand it or to verify it. There are resources available as books, software and web sites which will enable any intelligent inquirer to investigate the claims and data presented here. I will present these at the end of the book.

This book is not for everyone. It is written only for those who seek truth ,are open to new ideas , are capable of evaluating evidence rationally and forming logical conclusions.I hope you are in that category. Some will be inclined to accept before assessing the data, others may likewise be inclined to reject.Both parties will be wrong if they succumb to their biases because they will have missed the opportunity and pleasure of intense, thoughtful search and discovery, regardless the conclusion.

Prepare for a journey like you've never taken. If you have seen the movie, 'Contact', starring Jodie Foster, you can get an idea of the kind of journey I mean. There was an astro-physicist's intense search for truth, a coded message received from space, the decryption of the code, the building of the transport machine, and finally the journey.

I see many parallels between that story and this, hence my title, '<u>Divine Contact</u>'.

I have also seen hopeful signs of confirmation by the magnificent production of Mel Gibson's, "The Passion of The Christ". What is in my heart is almost beyond telling.

The story you are about to read is true.

Chapter One - A Personal Touch

I am a Protestant minister since 1976 and have devoted my waking hours primarily to studying the Bible in the original languages, not merely in sermon preparation , but because it holds a strong fascination for me ; a sort of spell hangs over it , and over me when I am studying it. I enjoy science, science fiction, working out, a wide variety of music and going to a drive-in movie (We have a couple drive-in's nearby). I love my wife and our twelve beautiful children and am extremely proud of and grateful for my family .

I was born to do a service for the world and that task is to bring forth the word of God. Every man has a service to render to the world.

It started at a funeral service in 1973. My best friend's younger 14-year-old brother had taken his own life in a manner that I will not detail. It was a very traumatic funeral scene for everyone. I was a pallbearer. I did not know the local minister officiating. I was not a religious person and seldom attended church. I was 20 yrs. old studying a Pre-Med program in the middle of my junior year at Rutgers University. I believed in God and believed that one should not take The Bible literally or seriously. My beliefs had not prepared me for what was to follow.

The minister read a verse from Deuteronomy – "***Oh that they were wise, that they would consider their latter end***". He went on to ask where we would spend eternity and if we had considered it. He talked about Jesus Christ as the Savior of our souls and said that we needed to call on him for salvation. I can honestly say that I was not so much impressed with the words I heard as with an attending sense of power that gripped me; no , it was a Presence. Something moved me beyond the power of words to affect a person and beyond words to express what I was feeling and experiencing. There was strong crying and tears, and though just about everyone was crying , I sensed that others were not experiencing what I was.

I felt as if I had just evolved to a new and higher level. I was attuned to a new realm by a new set of senses . I now could see , hear and feel things , (or that) , which I never knew existed. It was as if I had just been created or transported to a new planet. I will attempt not to cheapen the experience with clichés and religious jargon .

I feel no need to preach or exhort you to pray or get religion or anything like that, because I did nothing to bring this experience upon myself. It simply fell on me. There is a Bible phrase that describes it in John's Gospel, chapter three , verse three . I will leave it to the reader to have a look. I simply tell you this because it helps to explain how my story starts and why.

By the way , that pastor is now my father-in-law. I left Rutgers the following semester and transferred the following academic year to a Christian university to train for The Christian ministry. I had met the minister's daughter there on my first visit to the campus. She was a campus tour guide. I fell in love with her the first time we met.

Divine Contact-The Original New Testament Discovered

My Quest for The Holy Grail of Holy Scripture

I was also on a quest for knowledge. I was driven to share what I had found- what had in truth found me - with as many as I could. I knew I must study the Bible. I was in the grip of God.

While at seminary, I studied New Testament Greek and became fascinated with Textual Criticism – the science of determining the original words of the Bible . There are thousands of Greek N.T. manuscripts , and all of them give the same story of Jesus' life, death and resurrection with minor variations. Ninety percent of them agree very closely even on the details of spelling and word order and are classified as the "Byzantine text" or Majority text. This is the group which I believed came closest to the original and probably contained within its more than five thousand manuscripts the original text of the New Testament.

I spent countless hours at the library studying Greek manuscripts and the different types among them. I did this on my own time and not as part of any course I was taking. I probably would have gotten better grades in my regular subjects if I had not been so obsessed with this egg-headed pursuit. I did become somewhat of an expert on New Testament texts , however. I had read just about everything written on the subject and even debated informally with a PhD. professor on the same .

I had always imagined the original New Testament might be discovered in a manuscript from the first century , unearthed from a cave, as were the Dead Sea Scrolls. As it turns out, the original was buried, not under the earth or in a cave, but under centuries of ignorance, obscurity and misinformation- perhaps deliberate misinformation.

The greatest surprise of this discovery to the western world would be that the original NT in its entirety was written , not in Greek, but Aramaic. Many may concede an Aramaic original for the Gospel of Matthew and perhaps Hebrews, as Eusebius and other early writers (Papias, Hesesippus) wrote of an original Aramaic Matthew and/or Aramaic Hebrews.

If such an Aramaic original were the case, why would the church from earliest times seem to pay no attention (in the West) to Aramaic manuscripts, but only to Greek ?

I have a theory, based on differences in the Greek and Aramaic mss. themselves. The details I shall discuss later, but the theory I present here.The early church believed , understandably, that the original text was divine in origin and most holy, to be preserved intact at all costs.The entire Aramaic text was translated into Greek, under the auspices of the apostles themselves, for the Greek speaking Roman nations, as Greek had been the "Lingua Franca" (common language) of the Roman Empire since Alexander's conquests of 330 BC. (There were exceptions to this trend, however, in Israel and the Middle East (Asia Minor) , Aramaic had been established since the Babylonian and following Persian Empires as the common tongue. The Roman conquests did not include the Assyrian people of Mesopotamia or other "Barbarians" (so called by the Greeks) of the Aramaean people in what is now known as the Middle East.

The Greek translation served a double purpose. **It provided the Western world with the gospel message** and teachings of The Christ and His Spirit through the apostles **and it served as a decoy** – a camouflaged original that would deflect attention and attacks from Christianity's many powerful enemies , including the Caesars , from the Aramaic original manuscripts to the Greek manuscripts.The Eastern Assyrian Church, of course, never gave credence to this ruse of a Greek original.

If this was the strategy of the early church to protect the New Testament, it apparently worked pretty well. Many controversies raged over the Greek mss. and different readings cropped up among them , some no doubt being deliberately inserted to support or oppose certain doctrines. There are an estimated 100,000 variant readings among the major text types of **the Greek NT**. *A variant reading is a reading in a New Testament manuscript that differs from most manuscripts.*Most are quite minor and do not affect the sense of the text, nevertheless, still thousands remain that do.Thankfully , there are thousands of Greek mss. available , 99% of which are in close agreement with each other and bear excellent witness to the original text.

I have learned that Aramaic was the official tongue of commerce and the common tongue of the Persian, Babylonian, Greek and Roman empires for the nation of Israel and surrounding Semitic nations. This continued from the 7th century B.C. to the 8th century A.D.

I knew that Aramaic was the language of Jesus and his disciples but I also "knew" (by conventional Biblical scholarship) that Greek was the language of the original New Testament. Then I read the following from Josephus, the famous first century Jewish historian of the nation of Israel,certainly one of the most highly educated men of his time:

"I have also taken a great deal of pains to obtain the learning of the Greeks, and to understand the elements of the Greek language, although I have so accustomed myself to speak our own tongue , that I cannot pronounce Greek with sufficient exactness. For our nation does not encourage those that learn the language of many nations. On this account, as there have been many who have done their endeavors, with great patience , to obtain the Greek learning, there have hardly been two or three who have succeeding herein , who were immediately rewarded for their pains." – Antiquities XX, XI 2.(published circa A.D. 93)

The above quote from Josephus shows three things:
1. The language of the Jews of first century Israel was not Greek; it was not even a second language, as it had to be studied to be understood.
2. Very few of Josephus'countrymen had studied Greek enough to become fluent in that language and to find it profitable.
3. Greek education was not encouraged in Israel.

In A.D. 77, Josephus wrote his Jewish Wars in Aramaic and translated it into Greek for the Greek- speaking Roman citizens. Even his later *Antiquities,* quoted above,shows that Josephus was not fluent enough in Greek to compose his several volumes in that language. The Jewish rabbis of that time forbade the teaching of pagan tongues to their young men. They taught that it was preferable to feed one's son the flesh of swine than to teach him Greek.

Josephus also published the following in AD 77:

1. 1) Whereas the war which the Jews made with the Romans hath been the greatest of all those, not only that have been in our times, but, in a manner, of those that ever were heard of; both of those wherein cities have fought against cities, or nations against nations; while some men who were not concerned in the affairs themselves have gotten together vain and contradictory stories by hearsay, and have written them down after a sophistical manner; and while those that were there present have given false accounts of things, and this either out of a humor of flattery to the Romans, or of hatred towards the Jews; and while their writings contain sometimes accusations, and sometimes encomiums, but no where the accurate truth of the facts; I have proposed to myself, for the sake of such as live under the government of the Romans, to translate those books into the Greek tongue, which I formerly composed in the language of our country, and sent to the Upper Barbarians; (2) Joseph, the son of Matthias, by birth a Hebrew, a priest also, and one who at first fought against the Romans myself, and was forced to be present at what was done afterwards, [am the author of this work].

Divine Contact-The Original New Testament Discovered

In the above Prelude to His "**Wars of The Jews**" ,Josephus informs the reader that his works were not composed in Greek, but translated into Greek from "the language of our country", and that the original language text was sent "to the upper barbarians", which is generally accepted as a description of the Aramaic speaking Babylonians, Persians,Syrians and Mesopotamians.

This testimony of Josephus also establishes three things:

1. Greek was not the language of his country, Israel.

2. Hebrew was not the language of his country. The Barbarians did not speak Hebrew;they did speak Aramaic.Aramaic had been the lingua franca (common tongue) of the Middle East and Asia Minor for many centuries and would continue so for may more.

3. Aramaic was the language of Israel at the time.

If The Jews in Israel spoke and read Greek, why would he say , "**I have composed the books in the language of our country and proposed to translate them into Greek**"?

Would it not have made sense to simply write the original in Greek ? Everyone would have been able to read his works, both Jews and Gentiles of Rome. Obviously, Josephus testifies that Greek was not the language of Israel and that Hebrew was not the language of Israel. He also testifies of Israel as monolingual, not bilingual- "The language of our country", not "one of two languages of our country".

This naturally raises the question : What is the language of the original NEW TESTAMENT ? I and thousands of men and women in the ministry have learned that Greek is the original language of The New Testament. We have thousands of Greek NT mss. reaching back to the early 2nd cent. A.D.*(AD 125 is the earliest Greek NT manuscript portion)* ,witnessing certainly to the probability that there were Greek manuscripts of The NEW TESTAMENT in the first century.

(to *you)* לכון (I) אנא (say) אמר (for) גיר (Amen) אמין

(& the Earth) וארעא (Heaven) שמיא (will pass away) דנעברון (that until) דעדמא

(will pass away) נעבר (not) לא (Taag) סרטא (one) חד (or) או (one) חדא (Yodh *) יוד

(will come to pass) נהוא (everything) דכל (until) עדמא (The written Law) נמוסא (from) מן
-Matthew 5:18 (Bauscher's Aramaic-English Interlinear Gospels)
(Aramaic reads right to left)

"Amen, I say unto you, that until Heaven and Earth pass, one Yodh or one Taag will not pass away from The written Law until everything comes to pass." – Our Lord Jesus Christ (Maran Yeshua Meshikha)

- *"Yodh" is the smallest Hebrew letter. A "Taag" is a crownlet written above certain letters by the scribes and preserved in The Hebrew Massorah (scribe's notes) to identify certain significant words and their usages and number of occurrences in the scriptures.This indicates that the Hebrew scriptures would be Divinely preserved via the meticulous work of the Hebrew scribes, and that the Massoretes of the sixth century AD were carrying on a tradition that existed in the first century and earlier, as referenced here by our Lord.*

Why and how would Jewish men of 1st century Israel write accounts of Jesus' life for their countrymen in the Greek language ? First of all, could they, and then, if they could, would they? If they had done so, would the people have been able to read such gospels? The answers to these questions are really one resounding "**NO**", in my mind.

Does anyone have a better history of that time than Josephus ? **Josephus is practically the history of that time , along with THE NEW TESTAMENT itself** , and The NEW TESTAMENT itself does not directly state in what language it was originally penned. It can be examined for Aramaic and Greek terms to see whether evidence exists to show one being translated into the other , though I suspect one can produce a case supporting either side of the question. Historical evidence is probably more decisive in this arena.

There is another approach to this – another sort of internal Biblical evidence, but more on that shortly.

CHAPTER 2
Enter The Peshitta

The Peshitta (pronounced "Pe-**sheet'**-a")is the ancient Aramaic Bible, containing both the Old and New Testaments. **Aramaic is generally acknowledged to be the language that Jesus and His countrymen spoke.Aramaic is very similar to Hebrew. It shares the same alphabet and grammar.Many words are the same or very similar in both languages. Hebrew and Aramaic are called sister languages. Portions of The Hebrew Old Testament (half of Daniel and Ezra 4:8-6:18) are written in Aramaic.**

The New Testament Peshitta is supposed to be a 2nd century translation of the original Greek New Testament . **There is mystery surrounding it, for although it is considered the earliest and best version, no one can find any account of its translation or time period.**In light of Josephus' statement above quoted, and the fact that he, a highly educated Jew and Roman citizen of the first century, wrote his history of the Jewish Wars in Aramaic, **it is completely illogical to presume that Jewish apostles wrote the New Testament in a language (Greek) that they did not know, for their own people, the Jews, who did not understand it**. There is also the obvious contradiction of history.

Some may argue that God miraculously enabled them to do that very thing and the people miraculously understood it. I read of no such phenomenon in The New Testament. The gift of tongues was a gift of speech and not of writing and reading. At Pentecost, people of all nationalities heard the gospel in their own tongue as the apostles spoke. It was a gift to the apostles, not the masses. It certainly (Acts 2) does not say that the apostles ever wrote Greek gospels and that the Jews obtained the ability to miraculously read Greek from that day on. That would have guaranteed the conversion of all the Jews to Christianity, which we know did not happen.

The evidence supports the idea that THE GOSPELS were written originally in the language of the Jews, which was Aramaic, and later translated into Greek, the language of the Roman Empire.

Jesus instructed the apostles to go first to Jerusalem , all Judea, Samaria, and then the uttermost part of the earth .- Acts 1:8. **History confirms that this was the order of missionary activity. The Jews were the first to hear, and many of them did believe(See Acts 6:7) . The church at Jerusalem was the center and birthplace of Christianity. See Acts 8:1-4,31. What missionary takes no Bible and gives no Bible to the people to whom he or she ministers? The people need the written word to sustain the preaching of the word. Aramaic was the language of the people**.

Divine Contact-The Original New Testament Discovered

I have been so inspired with the knowledge I am about to divulge that I have undertaken to translate an **Interlinear Aramaic-English NT** and a prose translation afterward. I have already completed The four Gospels and have published them. There has not been a complete interlinear done yet of **the Peshitta NT**, nor a modern translation of it that is satisfactory, in my view. I have a few sample verses of the interlinear in this book to give an idea what it looks like and of its relevance to NT studies.

History of The Peshitta

The Peshitta ("*Pe-sheet'-a*") is the official Bible of the Church of the East. The name "**Peshitta**" in Aramaic means "**Straight**', in other words, the original and pure New Testament. The Peshitta is the only authentic and pure text which contains the books in The New Testament that were written in Aramaic, the Language of Meshikha (the Messiah) and His Disciples.
The Peshitta Old Testament is acknowledged to be a translation of The Hebrew Bible, and is not the original Old Testament. The Peshitta New Testament is viewed differently.

In reference lo the originality of The Peshitta NT, the words of His Holiness Mar Esha Shimun, Catholicos Patriarch of the Church of the East, are summarized as follows:

'With reference to-.. the originality of The Peshitta *text, as the Patriarch and Head of the Holy Apostolic and Catholic Church of the East, we wish to state, that the Church of the East received the scriptures from the hands of the blessed Apostles themselves in the Aramaic original, the language spoken by our Lord Jesus Christ Himself, and that thePeshitta is the text of the Church of the East which has come down from the Biblical times without any change or revision."*

Mar Eshai Shimun

by Grace, Catholicos Patriarch of the East April 5, 1957 found at:http.www/ peshitta.org

As far as I can tell, no such claim is made for any other ancient New Testament text.
I would never have accepted such a statement concerning The Peshitta text until 2002 , when I found mathematical evidence via computer which supports it.

Chapter 3
What is A Bible Code ?

At my request , Kevin Acres sent me an edition of the Aramaic Peshitta version of The NEW TESTAMENT for Codefinder and a copy with a scrambled control text as well. I immediately went to work, searching it for the most significant and likely candidate for a "NEW TESTAMENT CODE" I could think of.
I must explain what I mean by "NEW TESTAMENT CODE". There are books , articles , movies and even TV documentaries on the subject of "Bible Codes". The Omega code I & II are two movies that portray Bible codes. Michael Drosnin wrote a bestseller titled "The Bible Code" in 1996.Some of these productions are good and some not so good, but most of them will give a fair idea of what a Bible code is supposed to be.

Divine Contact-The Original New Testament Discovered

A Bible code is supposed to be a hidden message in a Bible text. It is usually found by skipping a particular number of letters between each letter of the hidden message in the Bible text.

Here is an example of a "code" that can be found in any English text of considerable length; It is not statistically significant or meaningful in any way, but it illustrates how a true code might be hidden and found in a text.

Even him, whose coming is after the working of Satan with all power and signs and lying wonders,
Even him, whose coming is after the working of Satan with all power and signs and lying wonders,
This is 2 Thessalonians 2:9 from The King James Version of The New Testament.
Starting with the first **L** in "all" and counting every third letter to the right, three times, spells the word, "Lord". This is not unusual for a short word of four letters. The software program, "Codefinder", calculates that by skipping 2 to 10 letters, a search for the word "Lord" should find 41 occurrences by chance alone in the KJV New Testament.
If I search The English text King James Version NT for the name "Jesus Christ" as a code at possible letter skip of 2 through 100,000 letters, Codefinder software calculates the chance of finding one occurrence as one ten thousandth, or 1 in 10,000. I have searched for this name as an **ELS** (*the term means "Equidistant Letter Sequence" and refers to a term being searched as a "code" which may be hidden in a text by skipping a consistent number of letters in the text*), and this name does not show up as an ELS in The King James Version of The New Testament.
If I flip a coin 5 times and get heads every time, that is not nearly as meaningful as if I flip a coin 100 times and get heads every time.So the more searches I do, the more meaningful the results, all else being equal.Each letter in a code, or ELS , is like another flip of a coin. Finding a ten letter ELS in The New Testament is roughly like flipping a coin ten times and getting tails every time. Beyond 10 letters, the odds generally increase exponentially at a much higher rate than coin flipping. See chapter 4 where I present the method for calculating the odds of a particular code. A twenty five letter code (the shortest long code presented in this book) is represented by the equivalent chance of flipping a coin 69 times and getting heads every time !

A longer ELS (skip word) has greater significance than a short one. A ten letter word is much more difficult to find ,by skipping letters ,than a four letter word.

 I chose to search the Aramaic book of Matthew for the Hebrew name of Jesus Christ.Hebrew and Aramaic have the same alphabet and use the same letters.I found nothing.

Then I did something that only Codefinder software would allow me to do ; I could set the program to "Search Wrap – On" , which would make any book or group of books a cylinder , O ,wrapping the end around and connecting to the beginning, so the search would continue when it reaches the end of Matthew at 28:20.

This modification produced a significant result. The name of Jesus Christ is expected to occur 0.054 times , based on letter frequencies of the text of Matthew for the corresponding letters of the name of Jesus Christ. That is a 5.4% chance. That in itself is not overly impressive. What is impressive is what is connected to the name before and after it.
Keep in mind that this was my very first search of The Peshitta . I focused on Matthew's Gospel. It yielded the first finding of a code in The New Testament that I am aware of. I looked at the resulting matrix and saw the following :

This is "Jesus Christ" in Hebrew, reading downward. There are more letters attached to either end:

The above long string of Aramaic letters shows in green,pink and blue letters what is attached to The Name of "**Jesus Christ**". The Codefinder program searched at all skip sequences from 2 to 20,000 letters. It found one occurrence at a skip sequence of **17,921 letters between each letter of the code.**

The English "code" example displayed above in 2 Thessalonians 2:9 (not a true code at all) has a skip of three letters –every three letters starting with the first **L** in "**All**" spell out the word "**Lord**". Just about anyone literate in English could compose a sentence with a similar ELS .(I will use the term "**ELS**" instead of "code", since the word "**code**" indicates the ELS ("Equidistant Letter Sequence") was intentionally put there, which needs to be proven.

An ELS with a skip of 17,921 , as found in Matthew, would not be so easy to compose. 17,921 letters is roughly nine chapters in Matthew. That means each code letter (and there are 61 of them) is spaced nine chapters apart from the next code letter , exactly 17,921 letters away ! Matthew has 57,798 letters, so this long code must cycle through Matthew (from beginning to end to beginning to end, etc.) , 18.6 times ! The whole code is presented here:

Chapter 4 - A Very Long Code Message in Aramaic Matthew

Bible Codes (צופני תנך)

Bible Codes In The Peshitta Version of Matthew

This is the code without spaces in red letters:

לכדמדהנלכרתינרמיהבחלאיולנותובגאדתצלדנדמעבנורא יש ועמש יחבעגאדנלד

Below is what Codefinder displays as results for the search.

Skip	Start	End
17921	Matthew Ch 5 V 44 Letter 102	Matthew Ch 23 V 1 Letter 26

The ELS reference is 17,921 characters between rows.

There are 1 displayed terms in the matrix.

The matrix starts at Matthew Ch 5 V 44 Letter 102 and ends at Matthew Ch 23 V 1 Letter 26.

The matrix spans 1,075,261 characters of the surface text.

The matrix has 61 rows, is 1 columns wide and contains a total of 61 characters.

דנלד ... לכדמדהנלכרתינרמיהבחלאיולנותובגאדתצלדנדמעבנורא יש ועמש יחבעגאדנלד by itself makes no sense, because there are no spaces to form separate words. The code researcher (I was the researcher in this case) must attempt to separate the letters into Hebrew or Aramaic words by inserting spaces at appropriate places. This does not change the order or composition of the skip text found, but is necessary to unravel the possible meaning of an ELS. I present my attempt at unraveling the letters in Hebrew below.

Hebrew-English Interlinear:

His women guests while I made sick from Jah of light to cut Me a covenant Behold ! a garment He seized

לכד מד הן לכרתי נר מיה בחלאי ולנותו

Part. Qal f.p.   Inf. Piel   Inf. constr   Perf.3ms Qal

1 Sam. 22:8 Root כרת
& 1 Kings 8:9, 2Chron 5:10

on a thick beam in blood Judging : In shadow steaming a delicacy

בג אדת צל : דן דם עב

cloud or beam in O.T. Part. sing. gen. constr. Part. sing. gen. constr.

of travail *on* a pedestal while was baking Messiah   Yeshua **(Jesus)** (was) terrible

נורא ישוע משיח בעג אדן לד

Lod -"Travail" Inf. Constr. Online Bible Heb. Lex. or Part. sing

לד – **"Lod" was the name of a city in Israel , meaning "Travail" or "Labor pains". It comes from the Hebrew verb "yalad" , meaning "to give birth", "to beget".**

Note: לכרתי above translated, **"to cut me a covenant" can also be translated, "for cottages". See Zeph. 2:6**

Hebrew reads right to left.The translation follows:

He seized a garment ,behold, to make me a covenant of light from Jehovah, while I made His women guests sick with a delicacy steaming in the shadow. Judging by blood on a thick beam was horrifying , while Jesus Christ was baking on a pedestal of travail.

This 61 letter code is from <u>The Peshitta</u> Version of Matthew and is my very first attempt to find a code in <u>The Peshitta</u> N.T. I used Codefinder 1.21 and had search wrap on , making this a toroidal search, going around Matthew 18.6 times , the skip being 17,921 ! The R factor is 66.98 for this one ELS !That translates to a probability of 1 in 10 to the 67th power (1 with 67 zeroes after it) in a text the size and letter makeup of the Aramaic gospel of Matthew.

A probability may be calculated using these two facts:

1.There are about 321 trillion possible ELS's in the entire Peshitta NT at all possible skip rates, from 2 to 461,094 letters (using wrapped searches).*[I obtain this from a formula in Ed Sherman's book,*

Breakthrough Discovery. Ed Sherman is a professional Statistician and proponent of Bible codes.His book is available at biblecodedigest.com.]

2. The isolated probability of a particular Hebrew or Aramaic ELS occurring at any skip number is

$22^{\text{neg. ELS length}}$. Example: If the ELS is 25 letters long, the probability of its occurrence is 22^{-25}, $1/22^{25}$.

22 to the 25th power is 3.63×10^{33}; one divided by that is written 2.75×10^{-34}, or 2.75 E-34 .

The probability of an ELS occurring in The Peshitta NT would be #1 (321 trillion) multiplied by #2.In the above example of a 25 letter ELS, the probability of its occurrence in The Peshitta NT would be 7.31×10^{-22}, or 1 in 10^{21}. That could be written 1 in 1,000,000,000,000,000,000,000, or one in ten billion trillion !

A scientific calculator or MS Excel can handle these large exponents.

For a 61 letter ELS, the calculation , 321 trillion times 22^{-61} is 4.15E-68, or 1 chance out of 2.4×10^{67}

#1 is based on The whole NT;The first code was found by searching only Matthew,therefore the probability is corrected to 1 in 5.34×10^{68}.

Just for the record, it should be noted that a ten letter ELS is very difficult to find in a text this size. The probability is less than one in a thousand for a straight search, without wrapping the text, end to beginning (called a toroidal search). Even with a toroidal search, the probability is only a few percentage points. This first Hebrew search was based on the phrase Yeshua Meshiach"-"Jesus Christ", which has a 5% chance of occurring as an ELS in Matthew.There are 53 meaningful letters attached to either end of the Name. How did they get there ?

[If Matthew had one letter more or one less, the above 61 letter code would not exist. The version of Matthew I used with Codefinder is from The Eastern Version, used by the Church of The East .]

I believe this code speaks of the Incarnation and Crucifixion of The LORD (Yahweh) Jesus The Messiah. The cloth "He seized" was the cloth of human flesh taken in His conception and birth of the virgin Mary through The Holy Spirit. The word, לכד, "seized" denotes violent victory over and possession of something or someone. God conquered the flesh of humanity when He took it on Himself , thus demonstrating complete mastery over temptation ,sin and the power of death.

The apostle Paul speaks of the body as a tent , which was woven of wool or camel hair. God transformed Himself -the Light of the cosmos - into human flesh and blood to become our Passover and atonement Lamb and our High Priest to take away the sin of the world. "Jah" ,The O.T. shortened version of **Yahweh** or **Jehovah**, Himself was the material of which the covenant was made , making it eternal , infallible , almighty and unbreakable.

"Wherefore when he cometh into the world, he saith, Sacrifice and offering thou wouldest not, but a body hast thou prepared me:Then said he, Lo, I come to do thy will, O God. He taketh away the first, that he may establish the second.By the which will we are sanctified through the offering of the body of Jesus Christ once [for all]." Hebr 10:5 ,9,10

God prepared a body for the Messiah before His entry into the world. The will of God is His New Covenant and that is consummated in the offering of the body of Jesus Christ once for all !

What , you may ask , is meant by , "The LORD made His women guests sick with a delicacy steaming in the shadow. ? The LORD (Yahweh) Himself was the One Who made the covenant ; The LORD was the One from Whom the covenant was cut (The material) and The LORD was the steaming delicacy (Living Bread)-

John 6:51, baking "on a thick beam" -"the pedestal of travail",under the darkness of God's terrible judgement against the sin of the world. The cross was the place where God's judgement was exhausted and the sin offering was consumed. Surely His women guests at the cross were sick in heart as they beheld this scene of the suffering of the incarnate God of Heaven.

Can you imagine Matthew picking a letter in chapter 5 verse 44,letter 102 (Lamed) and counting as he wrote his Gospel,17,921 letters forward to chapter 14, verse 11,letter 13 (Kaph) while he writes, another 17,921 letters forward to chapter 23,verse 18,letter 38 (Daleth), and repeats this count of 17,921 another 58 times as he writes his Gospel account,cycling through the book 18 times, spelling out the above 61 letter code of two sentences and 20 words ? I cannot imagine him doing this. Something else was going on here.

Now, take a deep breath; I'm just getting started

.

Chapter 5-Beautiful Christmas Code Emerges from Aramaic New Testament

Hebrew-English Interlinear:

in a manger Yeshua will blossom of God The Son where ? to lodge

להלן אהי בן אל יניץ ישוע באיבוס

The Aramaic language is very close to Hebrew, somewhat in the way that modern English is related to Shakespearean English, and in fact it uses the Hebrew alphabet. This code is expressed mostly in Hebrew, with the exception of one word, shown in red in the Hebrew spelling below.
The 25-letter code reads:

"**Where should the Son of God lodge? Jesus shall bud forth in a manger**."

Here's the Hebrew spelling: להלן אהי בן אל יניץ ישוע באיבוס

This code is an example of a "wrapped" ELS, where the text—in this case the entire Aramaic New Testament is made a loop, the end being connected to the beginning and searches can continue on indefinitely.

Note: This code has been verified by an Hebrew scholar fluent in the language- Dr. Nathan Jacobi.

This is an equidistant letter sequence- ELS, found using the computer program Codefinder 1.22 . It skips letters , searching for a code; in this case, I entered the words "Jesus in a manger", in Hebrew. It searched for the term in <u>The Peshitta</u> New Testament, which uses the Hebrew alphabet in its Aramaic language- The native tongue of Jesus and His countrymen.

The sense and symmetry in this code is unparalleled among other Bible codes I have seen which were found by others. It is poetic and powerful, as are all the codes I have found in The Peshitta New Testament. The imagery used here :Lodging The Son of God in a manger,Jesus budding forth as a flower in His birth, these are a signature poetic language found in all six of the long codes I have found and which I display in this book. They possess and convey a beauty rare among Christian and secular literature. All these codes also center around the Gospel story of The Messiah's birth, suffering, death and resurrection.

Codefinder 1.22 found the term , starting at Acts 27:10,letter 61, and <u>by skipping 18,474 letters</u> <u>backwards 24 times</u>, toward the beginning of the book, since this code reads backwards through the NT ,spelling out exactly what I have printed above. It ends at 2 Peter 1:2, letter 13 (James ,1&2 Peter follow Acts in the Eastern canon order of books) , after having gone back through Acts, John,Luke,Mark and Matthew, wrapping backward to the book of Revelation (15:3,letter 12) and continues backward to Hebrews,Philemon,1 Thess., Ephesians, 2 Cor. ,1 Cor. , Romans and stops at 2 Peter 1:2, letter 13 . 18,474 letters is about ten chapters of text.

How could such design and beauty be accidental ? That means there are approx. ten chapters separating each letter of the code, which code letters stretch essentially from Matthew to Revelation. There are exactly 18,474 letters between each of the 25 code letters !

Let's suppose that The Peshitta is a translation, as most scholars believe. It has existed for at least 1500 years. We have Peshitta manuscripts 1500 years old. The old versions, prior to 1905 did not contain 27 books as this version I have does. They had 22 books. But let's even grant 27 books to an hypothetical original Peshitta translation. How did a translator pull this off ? He had to write exactly 18,474 letters of translation between each code letter , a total of 24 times, reaching from 2 Peter 1:2,letter 13,where the code begins, to Revelation (which is not found in true Peshitta New Testaments) back to Matthew , Mark, etc. ,to Acts 27:10,letter 61. How could he do this, ensuring that his translation of the Greek NT would consist of exactly 18,474 letters from one book to another to the next code letter. To accomplish that one time would be an amazing feat;to do it 24 times in a row is very difficult , if not impossible to imagine. The fact that this code reads backward compounds the difficulty.

The Peshitta canon of the fifth century did not contain 2 John, 3 John, Jude or Revelation. It is ridiculous to posit a translator putting these codes in The Peshitta edition as it exists in the 27 book edition I have.

Then one must ask the question, "Why would someone do this?" ; and "Who would be able to find such a code ?" No known evidence exists that anyone left any record of writing or finding such codes in The Peshitta in The Eastern Assyrian Church or The Syrian Orthodox Church. There were no computers 1500 years ago to write such a translation, nor a computer to detect such codes.

If one letter of this 96% of The NT were deleted or one letter added to it, this Christmas code about The birth of Christ would not exist!

This particular version as I have it may not have existed in exactly this form, letter for letter, since the original NT manuscripts were written 1950 years ago. The mss. are extremely close in their texts, but there are some differences in many NT books. The critical edition was produced by comparing some 80 manuscripts and selecting the majority readings. Roy Reinhold then made some revision in a few places based on one or another group of mss. which added 50 letters to the total number in the 1905 edition. None of these codes exists in the 1905 version; none of them exists in The Eastern canon Peshitta; none exists in the standard Western edition.It is as if the codes were waiting for the 1905 edition to be edited in the year 2000 and analyzed by computer in the 21st century in order to be found.

Remember that the difficulty of composing a coded translation like described above increases exponentially when one considers that there are at least six long codes like the one above,and most are much longer than 25 letters. Three of the codes read backward; the longest and most recent finding is written in two languages (approx. half Hebrew & half Aramaic) and 23 letters of a 29 letter Aramaic section spell out a Hebrew code backwards !

 I have also found that hundreds of thousands of shorter Divine Name ELS codes exist in this text, far beyond what are to be expected to occur by chance.

What are the chances of finding this 25 letter message in this text?

Codefinder, using the frequency statistics for each letter of the code, calculates an R factor of 20, which essentially is the number of decimal places after the decimal point in the probability figure ! - 0.00000000000000000001 or 1 in 100,000,000,000,000,000,000 .
That is approximately 1 in 100 million-trillions.

Chapter 6-The "Revelation of Jesus" code in the Peshitta NT

our Lord   donned   of Yeshua   the revelation   I am ashamed

למרן   לבש   דישוע   גלינא   אבהת

for His tranquility Alas !   meditation about crushing Him   sprang up

לכושה   און   הגיא   בדשה   יעא

I am ashamed.
The revelation of Jesus clothed our Lord.
A plot to crush Him sprang up.
Alas for His tranquility !

אבהתגלינאדישועלבשלמרניאאבדשההגיאאונלכושה

Skip	R Factor (in Matrix)	Start	End
-99067	38.393	42.455	Hebrews 5:5.16 Acts 17:11.18

The ELS reference is 99067 characters between rows.
There are 1 displayed terms in the matrix.
The matrix starts at Acts 17:11.18 and ends at Hebrews 5:5.16.
The matrix spans 3863614 characters of the surface text.
The matrix has 40 rows, is 1 columns wide and contains a total of 40 characters.
There is 1 significant term in the matrix.
The matrix odds are $2.47156926329144 \times 10^{38}$ to 1 in favour of significance.
The cumulative 'R' Factor for the displayed matrix is 38.393.

I searched for the term, "גלינא דישוע" ("**The revelation of Jesus**") in **The Peshitta NT**. It consists of the first two words of the book of Revelation in The Aramaic Crawford manuscript which is used in The 1905 Critical edition of The Peshitta NT, also known as The Syriac Bible , published by The United Bible Society, 1979.The 40 letter code occurs once as an ELS, skipping 99,067 letters 39 times to find each letter of the 30 letter code attached to each ends of the 10 letter initial search term, as displayed above.

The initial search term , "גלינא דישוע" ("**The revelation of Jesus**") has a 3% probability (at skips of +-2 to +-100,000) of occurring in **The Peshitta NT** . There are 30 more letters attached , spelling out the above sentences in Aramaic. One word precedes the phrase, the other seven words follow it, forming a ten word Aramaic code of three sentences ! The composite probability is one in 10 to the 38th power ! This is not a likely scenario for a 2000 year old text written by any other than a superhuman intelligence !

Divine Contact-The Original New Testament Discovered

The code is found by connecting the end of Revelation to the beginning of Matthew , end to end, making the NT a circular string of 461,094 letters. The last letter of the code (ה) is at Acts 17:11, letter 18 (in Aramaic) and skips 99,067 letters to the next to last letter , (ש), etc. Each skip covers 21% of the NT text, so in the course of the entire search the Codefinder program cycles through the NT eight times plus !

Remove one letter from this Peshitta NT, and the code disappears ! The number of letters 461,094 in the 27 books is absolutely essential to the existence of this code. Remove one from any of its 27 books, and it all falls apart.

The matrix odds are **2.47 x 10^{38}** to **1** in favour of significance.

This is the second long code going through **The Peshitta NT** I have found. The other is a 25 letter code, covering 96% of the NT :

להלן אהי בן אל יניצ יושע באיבוס –
Where should The Son of God dwell ? Jesus shall blossom forth in a manger.

It also is a toroidal search , like the 40 letter code, cycling through Revelation back almost to the starting point at Acts 27.

Neither of these codes, or anything with even the initial two word phrase, occur in the Tanach control text (a scrambled text of The Old Testament).
The Christmas code was found by searching for יושע באיבוס ("Jesus in a manger) – a Hebrew term. The probability of this phrase occurring by itself (at skips of +-2 – +-100,000) , is **2%** in **The Peshitta NT**. The other terms are extensions of that phrase, discovered by reading the letters attached to the string of letters following it, letter by letter, no spaces between ! The probability for the extended code of 25 consecutive letters in two very plain sentences is, one in 10 to the 20th power !

A test of **The Greek NT (1550 Textus Receptus, Tischendorf's 8th edition, The Byzantine NT, Nestle's Greek NT, Westcott & Hort's edition**, and even **Josephus' Antiquities in Greek** (1.63 million letters !) **shows** , when searching just for the one word , αποκαλυψις ("Revelation") – **absolutely nothing** ! At skips of +-2 – +-100,000 , the term has a 0.5 % probability of occurring in Josephus and 0.25 % in The Greek NT. No code exists in any of those texts with the word "**Revelation**" in it. Only The Peshitta NT has it. If the NT were to have codes in it, we should expect at least this word to be found as an ELS. The fact that it is not found in any Greek edition is quite a "**Revelation**" !

The Peshitta text has remained unchanged from the first century; all 350 manuscripts are essentially in uniform agreement. The Greek mss. are not nearly as uniform, even among the Byzantine and Textus Receptus traditions.
The Critical texts also differ; there is no settled tradition or standard. Every new Nestles or UBS edition has numerous changes from the 26 previous editions.

Commentary:

The code itself seems to be the thoughts of a disciple of our Lord – "**Maran**" ("**Our Lord**") , found in the code, is a title the disciples often used for Jesus (about 240 times), as written in **the Peshitta NT** .
"***I am ashamed***"-No doubt our Lord's disciples were filled with guilt about His crucifixion. They all abandoned Him during His last hours before His death.
"***The revelation of Jesus cothed our Lord***". It was pretty obvious that Jesus was more than a mere human being. He wore power as a garment and had control over nature, disease and death; His wisdom was limitless; He

seemed to know and be what only God could know and be, and His Spirit and glory manifested themselves on a mountain in a brilliance greater than that of the sun.

"*A plot to crush Him sprang up*"-They knew of the plots springing up to kill Him.

"*Alas for His tranquility* !"- I suppose they felt helpless to to do anything about it. He had warned them of His destiny; He was not a victim of circumstance or of His countrymen. He had willed it to be so for the sake of mankind's salvation. Even so, it was heart rending for them to stand by and behold . It would have been easier to turn away and wait it out. He had said He would rise again the third day.

Search Method:

I searched for the first two words ,"גלינא דישוע" ("**The revelation of Jesus**") of the Book of Revelation in Aramaic. The skip rates I entered were 2 to 100,000. The phrase only occurs once in this range , at -99,067 . A negative skip means that the term occurs backward in a forward search of the NT. The code's letters are found in 15 books , including the 4 Gospels, Acts, Romans, 1&2 Cor. , Ephesians, Philippians, Titus, Hebrews, 1&2 Peter and Revelation . The version I have searched here is the 27 book canon of the Peshitto, based on the critical editions of Gwilliams & Pusey for the Gospels , Gwilliams edition of Paul's epistles and Acts, and John Gwynn's critical edition of the minor Catholic Epistles and Revelation.

Even though the codes letters are not found in all the 27 books of the NT canon, the code relies on all the books having exactly the number of letters each one contains, or the code falls apart.

I have tried four editions of the Peshitta & Peshitto NT, as well as a scrambled text of the Hebrew Bible. None of them has any such code, not even the two word "Revelation of Jesus" phrase in Aramaic. This particular edition of the Peshitto uses the Eastern book order – *Matthew,Mark,Luke,John,Acts, James, 1 & 2 Peter, 1, 2nd ,3rd John, Jude, Romans, 1 & 2 Corinthians, through Hebrews, Revelation*. It was somewhat edited by Roy Reinhold , who supplied the Peshitto text for Codefinder, to conform to the Eastern Peshitto text in a few places , primarily in The Gospels. The differences are very few and minor. One version I tried is the 1905 Syraic NT. This version has 51 fewer letters than the Codefinder edition, which was edited from this version to conform more to the Eastern text, as just outlined above. The code does not exist in the 1905 edition; the two word phrase also does not occur there. The Eastern text 22 book Peshitta also has none of the coded information of the Codefinder edition. Another Western edition has about 50 letters more than the Codefinder edition's 461,094 letters. It also shows no such code nor the two word phrase on which it was built.

The same results apply to the 25 letter code I found in 2002. All this along with my Divine Names experiment, has led me to conclude that The Western Peshitto , in its critical edition, corrected somewhat to the Eastern text of The Peshitta, but containing the 27 books and the Pericope Adultera of John 7:53-8:11, is the original text of The New Testament, very nearly letter perfect ! All the evidence I have compiled thus far leads to the conclusion that **The Peshitta NT** in its present form was authored by God Himself !

Chapter 7- 61 letter "Man of The Tree" Code in The Peshitta NT

גיש בגעתה לרוח ומא לא שהללן מן יה לנש אילן לא דאמיתא פשיתתא הו אלו נחא שין להן

He was familiar in his cry to the Spirit . And who praised us not from Yahweh for the Man of the tree ? -not because He put to death The Pure One; It is -Oh that He would save (give life) , & reconcile (peace for) This One !   skip = -35348 ;R Factor in NT = 62.983 ;R Factor in Matrix= 66.861; Starts at-Hebrews 7:19.9; Ends at Luke 20:33.14

The above lines are output generated by Codefinder Software in a search of The Peshitta New Testament for a code (ELS) by skipping letters. I started with the phrase "The Peshitta is" פשיטתא הו , as highlighted in the Aramaic line below:

גיש בגעתה לרוח ומא לא שהללן מן יה
לנש אילן לא דאמיתא פשיטתא הו אלו נחא שין להן

An interlinear of the entire Aramaic code follows here: (Read right to left.)

Prayer for The Man of The Tree

(to The Spirit) לרוח (in His cry) בגעתה (He was familiar) גיש
(will praise us) שהללן (not) לא (& who ?) ומא
(of the tree) אילן (for The Man) לנש (Yahweh) יה (from) מן
(not) לא (because He put to death) דאמיתא (The Pure One) פשיטתא
(It is) הו (Oh that !) אלו (He would save) נחא
(giving peace) שין (to This One) להן

He was familiar in his cry to the Spirit .
And who will not praise us
From Yahweh for The Man of the tree?
It is not because He put to death The Pure One;
It is "Oh that He would save !
giving peace to This One !"

There are two irregularities in the spelling of this Aramaic code. One is שהללן , which has a proclitic –ש , not normally used in Aramaic, although it is used in Aramaic of Nerab and others-(See letter ש "Shin" entry in **Brown, Driver & Briggs Hebrew & English Lexicon**). The other is the absolute form of לנש אילן ("**The Man of the tree**") . I cannot find another place where this form is used ; the only cases for the absolute form of אנשא are "Bar-nash" – ברנש ("son of man") and Cal-nash – כלנש ("everyman"). In The Aramaic Targums of

The Old Testament, נש - "**man**"occurs always separate from בר - "**son**", in the same form as here. The latter irregularity is a one letter difference that conforms to the absolute form of "Enasha". It is recognizable as the word "**Enasha**" ("**Man**"). להן ("**This One**") occurs in The Targums several times as it is used here and in The Aramaic portions of Ezra and Daniel it means "**Therefore**" or "**except**".

This code is found in The Peshitta NT (1905 Syriac NT, critical edition as used in The Online Bible). Codefinder software distributor, Roy Reinhold, supplied me with The Peshitta module for that program, so I could search The Peshitta NT for codes. The Codefinder edition seems to have been slightly edited to conform with Eastern mss. in a few places where those differ slightly from Gwilliams' edition in the Gospels. The Codefinder edition has 51 more letters than Gwilliams' edition.

The code starts Hebrews 7:19 and skips **-35,348** letters each time to find the next letter in the code. It does this 60 times , cycling through the entire NT. It ends at Luke 20:33 , *but only after going through the NT 4.6 times altogether* in its search. The end and beginning of the NT are connected to make an endless loop. This is an optional setting in Codefinder called ,"Search wrap". Such a search is called a toroidal search, since the loop is a toroid. The R Factor of 62.98 at the top in blue is the exponent of probability that Codefinder calculates for this 61 letter code . *It means the odds against this sequence of Aramaic words occurring by chance are (10 to the 63rd power) to one !* Those are pretty big odds ! Another way of looking at it is that it means someone intentionally put this code in the text. It would have been someone of an extremely high order of intelligence, especially considering that it occurs only in this edited version produced in the year 2000 , the code reads backward from near the end of the ancient Peshitta canon (Hebrews is the last book of its 22 book canon) , proceeding toward the beginning, skipping some 35 chapters between each code letter. There are at least several other long codes like this and hundreds of thousands of short Divine Name codes occurring in highly significant numbers, far beyond the realm of chance.
I would like to see if anyone can find a code like this in The Greek NT. I and many others have been unable to for several years.
Long codes like this one (& I know of none in the Peshitta except those I have found) would disappear if one letter of the Codefinder edition Peshitta NT were deleted or one letter added !
The original search term was פשיטתא הו ,"**The Peshitta is**". "**Peshitta**" is an Aramaic word that means, "**Simple**", "**Right**", "**Pure**". It occurs twice in The Peshitta as an ELS between skips of -100,000 & 100,000.
Commentary:

"He was familiar in His cry to The Spirit" .

The code seems to recount our Lord's cry to God from the cross- "***My God, My God, why have you forsaken Me ?***"*The words had been written 1000 years before in Psalms 22:1. It was familiar to God because He also cried out from His Spirit for His dear Son.What Jesus uttered was the Soul of God in His Dying The Eternal Death- The Disintegration of The Triune Life of God (Father,Son and Holy Spirit). Each was dying (Death is separation) and crying out for the Other.This was truly The Divine death of* "***The Way, The Truth,The Life***"*.The Eternal Unity of God cannot exist without The eternal Threeness. If Christ The Son died, then the Godhead was rent asunder and the fullness of God in Christ also died. The Son ever was and is and shall be the Center and The One in Whom all The fulness of The Godhead dwells. If The Son dies, so The Father and The Spirit. Can you conceive of a greater love and sacrifice than this ?*
*"**There is no greater Love than this, than that a person would lay down his life for his friends.**"John 15:12*
The Peshitta (My Interlinear Translation)

Is The Love of Christ greater than the Love of God ? No , my friend, "***For God was in Christ,Who has reconciled the world with His majesty, not reckoning their sins to them***..."*2 Cor. 5:19 (Murdock's Translation). Christ is God Who offered Himself up completely , Body,Soul and Spirit , once for all, to put away sin. God did not give 33% of Himself; He gave it all ! Otherwise , any human hero could lay claim to a greater love than that of God The Father ! Perish the thought ! God The Father was hanging on the cross* with His Son and so was The Holy Spirit. Search you heart and mind; search 1 John 3:16 and consider the words: "**Hereby we perceive the love of God, that He laid down His life for us**..."Consider also these words:

"**Then answered Jesus and said unto them, Verily, verily, I say unto you, The Son can do nothing of himself, but what he seeth the Father do: for what things soever he doeth, these also doeth the Son likewise**". Joh 5:19

What was the greatest work Christ ever did ? He said He could do nothing of Himself. If He could not do a small deed without His Father, He certainly could not do the most difficult and important work without His Father. Did He do all the lesser works with His Father and then the greatest work without Him ? Surely His death was His greatest and most difficult work.

"He who has seen Me has seen my Father."

When did Christ appear most Divine and beautiful? Was it not on the cross ?Then it was on the cross that He showed us His Father most clearly- covered in His own blood .

"My Father and I – We are One."

Even in death ! Sundered from each other and Life's communion, yet One in nature and action; absolutely selfless and loving others more than His very Deity !

And who will not praise us
From Yahweh for The Man of the tree?

The second line speaks of the praise to God (The Triune God-"**Us**") of all people for the sacrifice of Jesus Christ. This speaks of universal worship and praise of God because of the atonement of Christ's death. "**From Yahweh**" indicates that the worshippers are in The Holy Spirit, as true worshippers worship God "**in The Spirit and in the truth**"- John 4:24. One must be **born of The Spirit** in order for that to happen-John 3:3-8.

"It is not because He put to death The Pure One"

The praise is not becauseJesus ("**The Pure One**") suffered and was put to death for us; it was really a praise for the love He demonstrated in willingly laying down His Divine Life for us all. There is no salvation in the ego- centric view of the cross of Christ. How could there be ?If we praise and thank God that He suffered and died "**for me**", we don't know anything about Him and salvation. If we could be primarily concerned for Him and pray for Him and His well Being, then we are truly saved.He did suffer for all of us, not just for me, and He suffered to save us from ourselves unto Himself.

It is "Oh that He would save !
giving peace to This One !"

There is strong pity expressed for our Savior and a prayer for His salvation from suffering on the cross. How many have felt so moved by sympathy for Him to so pray, but it is as if those watching Him die are praying for Him- a very beautiful and moving scene !
"**Amazing Love, how can it be, that Thou my God shouldst die for me ?**"-(Charles Wesley's hymn,"**And Can It Be ?**")

תשבוחתא לאלהא במרומא

Tishbokhta l'Alaha b'mruma

Glory to God in the highest !

Chapter 8 -The 88 letter "Messiah of Jehovah" Code in The Aramaic Peshitta New Testament

Hebrew –English Interlinear

This long version has 88 letters and employs a passive infinitive verb form of "Reeb"(to contend) not used anywhere in Hebrew Scripture:

city   from one   to be disputed   of The God   Son

בן האל להתריב מחד עיר

was spoken of by Me   bloody a firebrand He proposed a riddle He was lofty He was poor His night of Jehovah The Messiah caused to feel

המש המשיח יהוה לילו רש גא חד אוד דם ננמתי

with it of vapor & isle of vapor a companion of Jehovah from the isle you shall drive of The Stone & bitterness & religion & an index the interior I shall roam

ארוד גו וחו ודת ומר האבן תדף מאי יה בנת אד ואי אד בה

This shorter version deletes "The Son of God" and has the shorter noun form of "Reeb" (Contention) and has 80 letters:

was spoken of by Me bloody a firebrand He proposed a riddle He was lofty He was poor His night of Jehovah The Messiah caused to feel city of one the contention

ריב מחד עיר המש המשיח יהוה לילו רש גא חד אוד דם ננמתי

with it of vapor & isle of vapor a companion of Jehovah from the isle you shall drive of The Stone & bitterness & religion & an index back I shall roam

ארוד גו וחו ודת ומר האבן תדף מאי יה בנת אד ואי אד בה

[For The Son of God to be contended against], *or* [A contention] from one city caused The Messiah of Jehovah to feel His night; He was poor, He was lofty; He proposed a riddle: "A firebrand of blood was spoken of by Me. I shall roam back , & an index , religion, & the bitterness of 'The Stone' you shall drive out from the isle of Jehovah, a companion of the vapor & isle of vapor with it".

This code, like all the others I have found , seems to be poetic in form, therefore I display it in verse below:

The Night of The Messiah

City   from one   to be disputed   of The God   Son

בן   האל   להתריב   מחד   עיר

His night   of Jehovah   The Messiah   caused to feel

המש   המשיח   יהוה   לילו

He proposed a riddle   He was lofty   He was poor

רש   גא   חד

was spoken of by Me   bloody   a firebrand

אוד   דם   ננמתי

of The Stone & bitterness & religion & an index   the interior I shall roam

ארוד   גו   וחו   ודת   ומר   האבן

of Jehovah   from the isle   you shall drive

תדף   מאי   יה

with it   of mist   & isle   of mist   a companion

בנת   אד   ואי   אד   בה

For The Son of God to be contended against by one city

Caused The Messiah of Jehovah to feel His night

He was poor, He was lofty, He proposed a riddle:

"A firebrand of blood was spoken of by Me.

I shall roam the interior,

And an index, religion, and the bitterness of 'The Stone'

You shall drive out from the isle of Jehovah,

A companion of the mist and isle of mist with it".

The longer version analysis:

Skip	R Factor	(in Matrix)	Start	End
70328	95.163	98	Acts Ch 19 V 21 Letter 22	Ephesians Ch 2 V 2 Letter 13

The ELS reference is 70328 characters between rows.
There are 1 displayed terms in the matrix.
The matrix starts at Acts Ch 19 V 21 Letter 22 and ends at Ephesians Ch 2 V 2 Letter 13.
The matrix spans 6118537 characters of the surface text.
The matrix has 88 rows, is 1 columns wide and contains a total of 88 characters.
There is 1 significant term in the matrix.
The matrix odds are 1 chance in 1.45490828245436E95 in favour of significance.
The cumulative 'R' Factor for the displayed matrix is 95.163.

Shorter Version:

Skip	R Factor	(in Matrix)	Start	End
70328	85.867	89.628	2 Corinthians Ch 3 V 3 Letter 56	Ephesians Ch 2 V 2 Letter 13

The ELS reference is 70328 characters between rows.
There are 1 displayed terms in the matrix.
The matrix starts at 2 Corinthians Ch 3 V 3 Letter 56 and ends at Ephesians Ch 2 V 2 Letter 13.
The matrix spans 5555913 characters of the surface text.
The matrix has 80 rows, is 1 columns wide and contains a total of 80 characters.
There is 1 significant term in the matrix.
The matrix odds are 1 chance in 7.36278434219578 E 85 in favour of significance.
The cumulative 'R' Factor for the displayed matrix is 85.867.

The original search term was המשיח יהוה -"Ha Meshiach Yahweh" – "The Messiah of Yahweh" or "The Messiah Yahweh". It has a 52% chance of occurrence in The Peshitta at skips +-2- +-100,000 with search wrap on.

This entire code is Hebrew and is found by skipping 70,328 letters at a time 79 times to find the 80 letter code. To complete the search, it cycles through The Peshitta NT twelve times. **If this Codefinder edition of The Peshitta NT had one letter more or less ,the code would disappear ! The same is true generally for the other four long codes I have found in The Peshitta.**This is the fifth long code I have found in The Peshitta NT and the longest one yet. Two are 61 letters, one is 41, and the Christmas code is 25 letters. There are undoubtedly more where these came from. All of them are about The Messiah; all but one about His suffering and death.

The grammar is fairly straightforward and the message is in riddle form, even explaining itself to be a riddle. I leave it to the reader to decipher the meaning.

The R Factor 85.867 is the Probability Exponent (10^{85} to 1) of the odds this string of letters is there by chance. The exponent of the number of electrons in the universe is 81- (10^{81}).
That gives an idea how great the odds are against this being a coincidence.

I challenge anyone to find such a code in The Greek NT or any other version of The NT.

Son of man, put forth a riddle, and speak a parable unto the house of Israel. Ezekiel 17:2

Chapter 9
A Bilingual – Bidirectional and Toroidal Aramaic NT Bible Code of 191 Letters !

Term Translation Skip R Factor   (in Matrix)   Start   End

צהיתהאילושדמיפכנותורנדמאמשתאאחרתאדעלמדעלמיבברברולעפרפאלאדודא
נתבאדונברנשמחאנההמתאדתאלאינואהדדלבאתכבעאטטרנהו

-----   74806   108.121   111.794   Ephesians Ch 1 V 16 Letter 35   Acts Ch 20 V 15 Letter 35

The ELS reference is 74806 characters between rows.

There are 1 displayed terms in the matrix.

The matrix starts at Ephesians Ch 1 V 16 Letter 35 and ends at Acts Ch 20 V 15 Letter 35.

The matrix spans 7256183 characters of the surface text.

The matrix has 98 rows, is 1 columns wide and contains a total of 98 characters.

There is 1 significant term in the matrix.

The matrix odds are 1 chance in $1.32253634146643E108$ in favour of significance.

The cumulative 'R' Factor for the displayed matrix is 108.121.

This is a most unusual Bible code found in The Aramaic Peshitta NT. There are 98 letters forming Hebrew and Aramaic words. The initial search term was "חרתא דעלם" or "חרתא דעלם –Aramaic for "The end of the world" .

There are 93 letters forming Hebrew words and <u>77 of the same letters form Aramaic words</u>. <u>A 23 letter Hebrew code is found by reading an Aramaic code backward!</u> 21 letters are part of an exclusively Aramaic code. There are 191 letters of code in this 98 letter string! Connected to this 98 letter string are the following:

לוש דמי פכן ותורן דמא משתא חרתא דעלמי   29 lttrs   חרתא דעלמי משתא דמא ותורן פכן דמי לוש

(Aramaic) He kneaded my blood; He smote us and (stirred) shocked us , causing *us* to drink blood. *It was* the end of My world.

I have found this term ,"**He kneaded Me**" ,in another code in The OT. This term here probably refers to the communion cup and the bread being combined in ONE PERSON and sacrifice , as if blood were kneaded into the bread dough, symbolically. It also refers to the physical flagellation of our Lord; His blood and flesh were extensively intermingled. The "**drinking of blood**" would refer also to the cup at the last supper, from which our Lord also drank. We know from John 6:66 that our Lord's teaching about drinking His blood was a stumbling block to many of His followers, as they did not understand the spiritual meaning of His words.

It is the death of Christ that gives us life. To drink His blood is to draw life from meditation on His sacrifice of
    Himself in love to us- the sacrifice of His father in giving all that was His, which cup Jesus also drank, as
    He spoke of it in the garden of Gethsemane : "**Let this cup pass from Me**". He was not praying He might
    avoid death. He had come for the purpose of dying. He was praying for His Father, for he had known that

His Father was inseparable from Him, and would go to the very Death with His Only Son. Our Lord prayed not for Himself, but His Father and God. The Father gave Him the cup of His own blood also, signifying that he would also show His Son what to do by laying down His very Soul and Spirit first.

Jesus said , "**Verily, verily, I say unto you, The Son can do nothing of himself, but** what he seeth **the Father do: for** what things soever He doeth, these also doeth the Son likewise**.** (John 5:19) Do we believe these words, or do we think The Son of God was being poetic ? I can assure you, He was not poetic in His teaching. He was in earnest and taught eternal truth here, prefacing his words with the **double Amen**, in Aramaic, meaning, "**This is absolute , eternal truth**" . How did our Lord know how to die ? His Father showed Him; He died first. What could wrench the words of agony from The Eternal Son, always indissolubly One with His Father, "**My God, My God , why have You forsaken Me ?**" The Father could not watch His beloved die; He therefore died first, showing Him the way. And truly, they died as One together, as The Son lived by His Father and The Father's Life was His Son, Neither can exist without the other. Here is a beauty unsuspected by men in the eternal counsels. **For** the Father loveth the Son**, and sheweth him all things that himself doeth: and he will shew him greater works than these, that ye may marvel**. (John 5:20)

The death of our Savior was the greatest and most difficult work He ever did on behalf of mankind. Are we to believe He did this on His own, even though He expressly said he could do nothing on His own, but imitated what he saw His Father doing ? But as the blood was an offense to even many of the disciples, so is the idea that God The Father would lay down His life with his Son, to show Him the way in Love. Our Father is no mere spectator in the work of suffering and death necessary to save the world. He is no less a hero and Lover of Christ and men than His glorious Son is of God and the world of men.

With God's death, all men died. "*For the love of the Messiah constrains us to reason thus: One died for everyone; therefore everyone died with Him". Since Christ is The Divine Creator and Upholder of all things, and is eternally One with The Godhead, the creation perished with Him. And in His resurrection , all things were recreated new. "Whatever therefore is in the Messiah, is a new creation: old things have passed away; 18 and all things are made new, by God; who hath reconciled us to Himself by the Messiah, and hath given to us the ministry of reconciliation. 19 For God was in the Messiah, Who hath reconciled the world with his majesty, and did not reckon to them their sins; and Who hath placed in us the word of reconciliation." 2 Cor. 5:17-19.*

74806   25.696   29.369 Revelation Ch 2 V 17 Letter 6   Romans Ch 1 V 16 Letter 59

The following code is a reversal of the above Aramaic code in brown letters, read in Hebrew :

את שם אמד נרות ונכף ימד שוליא 23 lttrs

(Hebrew -read upward in matrix) The Alap Tau (Alpha - Omega) Name appraised lamps and epileptics measuring the hem of God. (Mat. 14:35,36)

-74806 16.309 19.981 Mark Ch 14 V 4 Letter 21   2 Peter Ch 2 V 1 Letter 25

In Revelation 1:8 of The Peshitta, את (**Alap-Tau**) is The name of **The Messiah** ,"**The Almighty**". I have uncovered evidence that The Greek NT translator interpreted this letter pair in at least 22 places in the NT as the title of **God** or **Messiah**, inserting those words into the Greek text where they did not exist in The Aramaic of The Peshitta, but the **Alap-Tau** (called **Aleph Tau** in Hebrew) combination did exist in a connected verb or noun. This study I have titled "**The Alap-Tau Codes in The Greek NT**". That same study also finds that the final יא - in The Peshitta NT in a few places was apparently similarly interpreted as "**God**" in the Greek text . Paul Younan , a native Aramaean,has commented that this ending can refer to "**Yahweh**" in Aramaic ; i.e. מריא- "**Marya**" means "**Lord Yah**" -יא – "**Jah**" or "**Yahweh**" & מר – "**Lord**". It has been established that מריא "**Marya**" is the Aramaic for "**Yahweh**".

If the last letter of the code be dropped, the last word means "**My hem**".

Both code letter pairs occur in the above Hebrew code which reads upward instead of downward like the rest. **Aleph -Tau** are the first two letters and **Yodh- Aleph** are the last two letters.

The **Aleph-Tau** ("Alpha –Omega" in Greek) of Revelation 1:8 walked among golden **lampstands** 1:12 , which are the seven churches – 1:20. Those are probably the "**lamps**" to which this code refers ; the "**appraisal**" or "**assessment**" is the evaluation of the churches by The Lord God Almighty ,The Messiah. The epileptic measuring God's hem is probably a reference to the healing power of Christ , according to Matthew 14:35,36: 35 (MUR) **And the men of that place knew him: and they sent to all the villages around them; and they brought to him all that were very sick; and they entreated of him, that they might touch at least the extremity of his garment. And they who touched, were healed.**

While the sick were testing the hem of God's garment, The Christ was assessing their faith by healing them through their faith.

One can imagine an epileptic touching the hem of Christ's robe and saying, **"Oh, I was only measuring it to make You a new one".**

בברר ולעף רפּא לא דודא נתב אדון ברנש מחא
נהמתא דתאלאין ואהה דלבא תך בעא טרן הו 61 lttrs

(Aramaic) In the natural state, & to multiply the flock, there shall be no trouble. The Lord shall sit as Son of Man to save . The hills *are* roaring and woe !-(a Hebrew word) - because the heart is wounded , He seeks His Rock.

74806   62.361   66.033 Ephesians Ch 2 V 15 Letter 6 Acts Ch 20 V 15 Letter 35

"**In the natural state**" follows "**It was the end of My world**" in the code. This would indicate that the sentence should read: "**It was the end of my world in the natural state.**" The first letter of "**In the natural state**" is found in Ephesians 2:15-" **Having abolished in his flesh the enmity, *even* the law of commandments *contained* in ordinances; for to make in himself of twain one new man, *so* making peace." KJV**

The "**natural state**" was **abolished** "in His flesh", (by His sacrifice), which means the old covenant of The Law was done away, and a new covenant was created. The natural state refers to the carnal nature of mankind apart from the spiritual life that comes by the new birth from the Holy Spirit.In this sense it was "**the end of the world**" , as a new order was established by which God would govern and relate to mankind.

Christianity grew swiftly and dramatically in the first three centuries. Augustine wrote in "The City of God" that the whole world was Christian in his time. He expected the golden age of a thousand years was soon to come or that they were in it. Persecution had generally subsided for the 4th through the seventh centuries, and the Roman Empire collapsed. There was also great missionary activity during that time. The Church of The East grew and spread as far as India and China from the Middle East in Persia. They became the largest Christian church in the world , having 100 million members. The Western church spread to Europe and went as far as Ireland , Scandinavia and Russia.

Whenever persecution did arise, our Lord would make intercessions for His people. Terrible persecutions did arise before and after the general period of calm. We must ever be mindful of those who suffer, as He is , for we are members one of another , brothers and sisters, and of the same body.

צהיתה איל ושד מי פכנו תורן דם אמש תא חרת
(First 2 are Aramaic; the rest is Hebrew) He thirsted for God, and a devil, who carved our vessel *and* a bloody mast last night in a chamber.

74806 27.926 31.598 Ephesians Ch 1 V 16 Letter 35   Romans Ch 9 V 5 Letter 5

The Christ said "**I thirst**" on the cross. He thirsted for His Father, for Whom he had cried out "**Elahi, Elahi, lemana shabaqthani**" ! A devil, or demon, would refer to a chief demon or Satan himself, who inspired the brutal whipping and torture of our Lord and the bloody crucifixion and cross (the mast) . All had been calmly carved (or inscribed) in a chamber the night before, even down to which cross He would be nailed to (perhaps it was newly cut wood). He is our ark of safety , carved and battered as the ark of Noah by the storm of judgment, yet we are saved and safe within.

בברר ולעף רפא לא דודא נתב אדון בר נשמח אנה מתאדת 38 lttrs
(Hebrew) as he chose to fly . A mandrake did not heal a tracker .We made glad The Lord of The Son ; He mourned ; It (*The Spirit*) rose skyward.   74806   35.226 38.899
        Ephesians Ch 2 V 15 Letter 6 Ephesians Ch 3 V 19 Letter 16

A mandrake was a root in the shape of a man, believed to have magic properties. See note further down.

אל אין ואהה 9 lttrs
(Hebrew) "There was no God" ! And , Woe !
74806   -1.578   2.094   Revelation Ch 14 V 18
Letter 50   Luke Ch 12 V 8 Letter 62

This probably refers to the death of Meshikha. He had been reunited with His Father in Spirit, as indicated by His words, "Father, into Thy hands I commend My Spirit." They were again One in Life. To the disciples, however, God was dead. He had died and forsaken them, as they saw it. They of course did not understand how this could be, and they were overwhelmed with grief and despair.
The ELS reference is 74806 characters between rows.
There are 7 displayed terms in the matrix.
The matrix starts at Ephesians Ch 1 V 16 Letter 35 and ends at Acts Ch 20 V 15 Letter 35.
The matrix spans 7256183 characters of the surface text.
The matrix has 98 rows, is 1 columns wide and contains a total of 98 characters.
There are 7 significant terms in the matrix.
The matrix odds are 1 chance in 1.37004983905038E177 in favour of significance.
The cumulative 'R' Factor for the displayed matrix is 177.137.

The End of My World
חרתא דעלמי

tracker mandrake not healed
רפא לא דודא נתב
My blood He kneaded
לוש דמי
& stirred us He smote us
פכן ותורן
To drink blood
דמא משתא
God He thirsted for Him
צהיתה איל
& a devil
ושד
of blood & mast our vessel who
מי פכנו תורן דם
carved *in* a room last night
אמש תא חרת

to fly also he chose

בברר ולעף

in the natural state of My world the end

חרתא דעלמי בברר

it shall be calm the flock & for multiplying

ולעף רפא לא דודא

to save *as* Son of Man The Master shall sit

נתב אדון ברנש מחא

& woe ! of the hills   the roaring

נהמתא דתאלאין ואהה

was wounded for The Heart

דלבא תך

His Rock He sought

בעא טרן הו

we gladden of The Son The Lord

אדון בר נשמח

He ascended He mourned

אנה מתאדת

Woe ! was not God

אל אין ואהה

lamps appraised Name Alap-Tau

את שם אמד נרות

the hem of God measuring & epileptics

ונכפי מד שוליא

מד is an infinitive construct from מדד.

The End of The World

A mandrake did not heal the Tracker

He kneaded my blood

He smote us and stirred us

To drink blood

He thirsted for God

While a Devil

Who carved our vessel

And a bloody mast

Last night in a chamber

Chose also to fly

It was the end of My world in the natural state

And to multiply the flock,

There shall be a calm

The Lord shall sit

as Son of Man to save

The hills are roaring and woe !

Because The Heart is wounded

He seeks His Rock

We make glad The Lord of The Son

He mourned – He (The Spirit) ascended

There was no God, but Woe !

The Alpha-Omega appraised lamps (Rev, 1:8,12,20)

And epileptics would measure the hem of God (Mat. 14:35,36)

Commentary:

I take the primary subject to be the Christ in this code. The speaker could be a disciple ,God The Father , or Christ; it is hard to tell, and the speaker may change from one sentence to the next. All of it seems to relate to the gospel story.

I would describe the codes I have found thus far as allegorical poetry or poetic allegory. Powerful imagery and metaphors are used to convey a profound message and story- the story of the gospel of Jesus: The Last Supper, His prayer to His Father in the garden of Gethsemane ,His scourging , His cross and cry to God, His ascension to Heaven and even His appearing in glory to His apostle John, walking among His church. He is also presented as the healer of those who can reach the hem of His garment by faith.
At first it strikes one as strange, but I find a strange beauty and symmetry in the words and theme, centering always around The One Person and story.

At my wife's suggestion, I have arranged the seven sections of code into a more chronological order , though there are still flashbacks in the narrative that may seem disjointed.

A mandrake (a man shaped root with supposed healing powers) may refer to Jesus Himself, Whom Isaiah calls "a root out of a dry ground" in his prophecy of Isaiah 53 , written 700 BC. This "Root" was a Man! The "Tracker" is also Jesus. He came "to seek and save that which was lost"; yet He could not save Himself, as the priests said of Him as He hung on the cross, dying: "He saved others, yet He cannot save Himself." Thus a paradox is presented, which the gospel account represents- God became a victim, even a sacrifice. He Who healed thousands with His word and hand allowed His hands and feet to be spiked to wooden beams to hang and die, for it was in refusing to save Himself that He saved the world, "and with His stripes we are healed". That is why we love Him; He demonstrated such incredible love for us all in laying down His Divine Life and Person to win our hearts and souls back to Himself and His Father God. And "our God was in The Messiah , reconciling the world unto His majesty, not imputing their sins to them."-(2 Corinthians 5:19 from The Peshitta text.)

There on that cross hung all of the fullness of Deity and Heaven, dripping with His own blood, which was shed for our sakes. Never sat more regal a king on a throne than this King upon His cross; never more glorious a crown adorned a human brow than the crown of thorns pressed into His scalp. Never from so majestic a throne reigned any potentate as This Man bloodied, beaten, mocked and rejected by all men , reigns from that cross over all people of all nations of all the ages past and yet to come- This King of kings and Lord of lords. There has never been His like, nor ever shall be- our Yeshua, The Savior - Lifegiver and Lover of our souls.
See His glory there on that cross in the darkness that darkened the sun and all the earth while the Light of the world was going out. Never has darkness radiated such glorious brilliance, which though blinding, makes blind men see. Never was seen such strength as in the weakness of His dying, nor such an infinite Life in Death. I call it "The Supernova of The Son". A supernova is the sudden burst of energy and light – a several billionfold increase in size and brightness in a star just before it dies.

And there died The Life, The Truth, The Way-The Eternal God;Spirit, Soul and Body.

Impossible, you say ? Yes, of course, but when did He ever let the impossible stop Him ? There was no other way to save us than this way. He majors in the impossible. Nothing is impossible with Him.

"There is no greater love than this, that someone would lay down his life for his friends."

Shall we say that God our Father had not the greatest love possible ? Shall we infer that He has spared Himself while sending His Child to suffer and die ? Heaven forbid it ! He Himself was always present in His Son and was and is eternally inseparably united with Him , in Life and in death. Therefore the death of The Christ was the death of The Triune Godhead- a primarily Spiritual and eternal event revealed in time , space and matter, in the crucifixion of Jesus' body on a cross in Jerusalem AD 30, on a hill called Golgotha and Calvary. <u>That death marked the end of the world</u>.
And <u>the resurrection (also primarily a spiritual and eternal event) marks the beginning of a new creation – A New Heaven and a New Earth, which are eternal</u>.

14 For the love of the Messiah constrains us to reason thus: One died for everyone; therefore everyone died with Him. 15 And He died for all, that they who live should not live to themselves, but to Him who died for them and rose again. 16 ¶ And therefore, we know no person after the flesh: and if we have known the Messiah after the flesh, yet henceforth we know Him no more. 2 Cor. 5:17 "Whatever therefore is in the Messiah, is a new creation: old things have passed away; 18 and all things are made new, by God; who hath reconciled us to Himself by the Messiah, and hath given to us the ministry of reconciliation. 19 For God was in the Messiah, Who hath reconciled the world with his majesty, and did not reckon to them their sins; and Who hath placed in us the word of reconciliation." (My revision of Murdock's Translation of The Peshitta 2 Cor. 5:14-19)

The Messiah is God The Omnipresent; what part of creation does He not contain, Who fills all in all ? This translation of The Peshitta is more accurate than the translations of the Greek NT. <u>There is no "if" in the</u>

text. The universe is entirely new because its Creator died and ended all things in His death. He arose and made a new creation in His resurrection.

We ought to therefore adjust our view of the world as Paul said he did: "And therefore, we know no person after the flesh." "Everyone died with Christ's death", says Paul. "All things are new". We must not think carnally about the world; we must think spiritually, that is we must be guided by the word and Spirit of God and by faith in His revelation of His works.

We live now in a New Heaven and a New Earth; we shall see it as such when we believe it. Therefore let us , as Paul, think of no man in the flesh, but as in the risen , ascended Lord Yeshua The Messiah. This will change the minds and hearts of men. That is the will of God for us and all people.

This code is an incredible phenomenon , as are the other long codes I have found in The Peshitta, of 25 , 40, 61, 61, 88 letters each. This one totals 191 letters and is coded in Hebrew (93 letters) and Aramaic (98 letters), and has one Hebrew code formed by reading one 29 letter Aramaic code backward , resulting in a reverse 23 letter code.

The ELS reference is 74806 characters between rows.
There are 7 displayed terms in the matrix.
The matrix starts at Ephesians Ch 1 V 16 Letter 35 and ends at Acts Ch 20 V 15 Letter 35.
The matrix spans 7256183 characters of the surface text.
The matrix has 98 rows, is 1 columns wide and contains a total of 98 characters.
There are 7 significant terms in the matrix.
The matrix odds are 1 chance in 1.37004983905038E177 in favour of significance.
The cumulative 'R' Factor for the displayed matrix is 177.137.

The skip of this code is high , at 74,806, as are all the other long codes found. This one was found with Codefinder 1.23 Beta , using search wrap , making the Aramaic Peshitta NT search text a continuous loop by connecting the end of Revelation 22:21 with Matthew 1:1, thus allowing searches to continue around the New Testament practically indefinitely.
The search covers 7.2 million letters of text, which means it cycles through the NT 15.74 times , finding 6.2 letters average per each NT search !
I can think of no other code in which two languages (Hebrew & Aramaic) are paired to form codes as in this one, in which also another long code is found by reading the code string backward !

All the 7 terms are really part of one continuous string. The R Factor of 177 means that this set of Hebrew & Aramaic codes and the backward Hebrew code have a 1 in 10^{177} chance of being unintentional . That is a rather unlikely possibility.
Consider also the coherence and poetic style of this code with its integral theme of The Messiah's suffering , death and ascension. All the other five codes are also Messianic and are concerned with The Lord's birth (one code) and suffering and death (four codes).
Some will be disappointed that in spite of all the above evidence that The Peshitta NT was obviously extensively encoded by God with gospel information and that The Peshitta must be the original and Divinely inspired and infallible New Testament , there are no prophecies of current events.

I believe we all need to be reminded of the words of scripture in Revelation 19:10 "***Worship God: for the testimony of Jesus is the spirit of prophecy".***

I wish all preachers, Bible teachers and prophecy writers would learn the meaning of those words. All people need to learn it.

All Bible prophecy is about the testimony of Jesus The Christ. According to Yeshua, all the Messianic prophecies of the Old Testament (Luke 18:31) were fulfilled when Jesus went into Jerusalem for the last time to celebrate Passover , approx. AD 30, when The Lord God was arrested, put on trial, condemned to death, mocked and spit on, punched in the face, whipped , crowned with thorns, laughed at, given a cross to carry to Calvary and finally spiked, hands and feet, to that cross and left to die of a broken heart. He was then buried and He arose bodily on the third day. He appeared alive to over 500 people at one time, commissioned His disciples to preach The Good News to the world and disciple the nations, He ascended to heaven whence he came; He sent The Holy Spirit upon those waiting at Jerusalem, endowing them with Divine life and power to live and proclaim the words of their Lord and Messiah and to transform the world and build the church in all nations.

Luke 21:22 says that all prophecy would be fulfilled in the days of Jerusalem's destruction. That was accomplished in AD 70. The Book of Revelation starts out, "**The Revelation of Jesus Christ which God gave to Him**". The prophecy is called by His Name, for He is The subject of it. The Aramaic mss. of Revelation have a short prologue which says John was exiled to Patmos by Nero Caesar. Nero reigned from AD 54 to 68. He began a campaign of persecution against Christians in AD 64. I do not accept the late date of AD 95 for the date of Revelation. Revelation's prophecies were "**shortly to come to pass**" and "**the time is near**"; "**I come quickly**". These words point to a near fulfillment, not events 2000 years later. If the destruction of Jerusalem and the temple of God was "**the fulfillment of all that was written**" , as our Lord said, then we might expect a fuller account of that great event prior to its occurrence in AD 70.

The Roman siege of Jerusalem lasted three and a half years. This is the time frame repeated several times in Revelation of "**great tribulation**" and "**the treading under foot of the holy city by the Gentiles**". Our Lord prophesied that there had never been such great tribulation on the earth as would occur in Jerusalem's destruction. Josephus wrote that the Jews were starved , burned and shot with arrows & catapults and attacked with other weapons for over three years. Over a million Jews were killed- men, women and children by these most terrible and prolonged means of death, including diseases bred of rotting corpses. Revelation was written before these events occurred to warn the people of God to flee. What kind of warning comes twenty five years after the fact ? Revelation is an expansion of our Lord's prophecy in Matthew 24 and Luke 21 concerning the end of the nation of Israel and the holy temple and of the world as they knew it.

Chapter 10 – The Old Testament Messiah Codes

The first Bible Codes I discovered were in The Hebrew Bible (The Old Testament). Here is the first of them:

Bible Codes- צופני תנ״ך
Crucifixion of Messiah in Psalms 20-25

Term	Translation	Skip	R Factor (in Matrix)	Start	End

או יבאכוהיהממממוהויןנלאיהיצלעהשהיתגרישועמשיחי

| | | -45 | 40.795 | 44.079 Psalms Ch 25 V 7 Letter 16 | Psalms Ch 21 V 13 |
| | | Letter 28 | | | |

The ELS reference is 45 characters between rows.
There are 1 displayed terms in the matrix.
The matrix starts at Psalms Ch 21 V 13 Letter 28 and ends at Psalms Ch 25 V 7 Letter 16.
The matrix spans 1801 characters of the surface text.
The matrix has 41 rows, is 1 columns wide and contains a total of 41 characters.

nothing they shall be He vanquished them burning me it went on My desire (or Woe!)

אוי בא כוהי: הממם: והוין לא:

Aramaic vb. Dan. 5:17 2 Chron. 15:6 Part. w/pron. suff. Imperf. 3m.p. Peal Perf. 3m.p.Qal

my Messiah   Jesus a Stranger He shall be made shall be lame The LORD

יה יצלע : השית גר ישוע משיחי

Imperf. 3m.s.Niphal   Imperf. 3m.s. Qal

My desire went on burning Me. It vanquished them and they shall be nothing.
The LORD shall be lame.He shall be made a stranger- Jesus my Messiah.

This is an extension on my original central term in my Psalms 22 matrix. Can this message need explanation ? The ELS remains still within the parameters of the original matrix which centers around Psalms 22- the crucifixion Psalm. There is also the Mount formed by the words of my Messiah from the cross , "Eli, lama...", and "Mt. Moriah". The terms, "blood of God", "crucified", and "For the LORD Messiah saves" are all clustered around this long message.

This is the minimum skip (-45) for The name "Yeshua Meshiach" – "Jesus Christ", in the entire Old Testament.

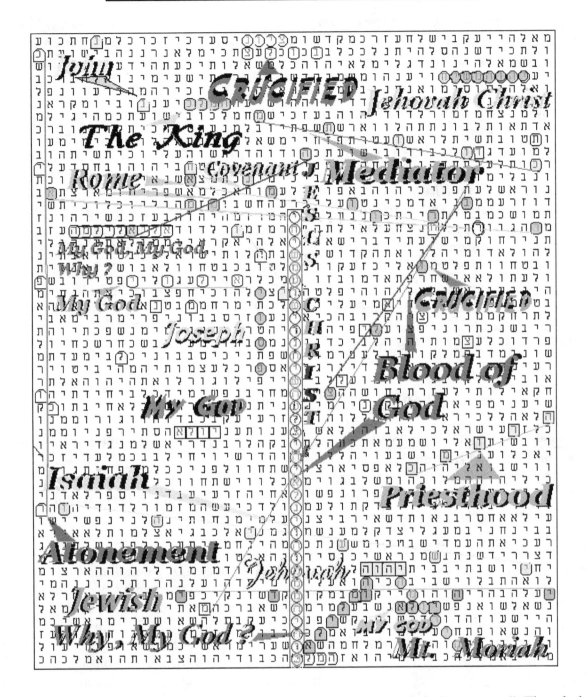

This matrix continues downward with 5 letters: אויבא, or אוי בא – "My desire went on". The whole message reads from the bottom upward.

According to Codefinder's computation of letter frequencies, the probability for this 41 letter string occurring by itself is less than 1 in 10,000,000,000,000,000,000,000,000,000,000,000,000,000,000.

Notice the Hebrew words "Eli lama" (My God, why?) & Mt Moriah at the bottom of the matrix form a hill with 2 – 45 degree angles with 6 letters for each side and at the top of that hill, four letters are centered perfectly, closing the gap between. Those four letters are יהוה (YHWH) "Yahweh", The most holy Hebrew Name for God. That is Who was on the top of that hill, Mt. Moriah, where Abraham took his son Isaac to offer him, and told Isaac, "God will provide Himself a lamb for a burnt offering". He called that place "Jehovah Jireh" –"Jehovah shall provide", and it was said for many centuries afterward, "On the mount of Jehovah He will be provided." (Genesis 22:14).

The whole area where the temple was built was Moriah, and our LORD was crucified on that same hill "The mount of The LORD", where they looked upon "Yahweh Whom they had pierced". Here it is in word and picture form in the Psalms as a matrix, centered in Psalm 22, the Psalm of the crucifixion of The Messiah. Coincidence ? Not very likely.

Considering the four coded sentences touching the side of this mount which speak of the suffering of "Jesus my Messiah" , at a skip of -45 (the minimum skip for "Jesus Christ" in the entire O.T.) touching a -45 degree angle side of a hill, which side is formed by the words in Hebrew of His very cry (Eli lama ?) from that very hill of suffering and sacrifice , "Moriah", whose name forms the other side of that hill, where prophecy said God would provide a lamb for a sacrifice, which words are found in that very Psalm 22 , around which the codes are formed, I would say that such a coincidence is impossible.
Wouldn't you ?

Chapter 11- The Message of the Codes

All the codes are about the Gospel of Yeshua Meshikha (Jesus Christ). God is calling us back to the simple and all powerful Gospel of His Son. Its words are eternal truth, the same yesterday, today and forever. They are "the things which are , and which were, and which are to come". They are about "Him Who is , and was, and is to come". Prophecy is not about what the newspaper reports. It is Eternal Truth that changes not- the same in every age to all people.

Let's reflect a bit on how these ELS's came to exist in this text. The most popular view of The Peshitta among Western scholars is that it is a translation made in the early fifth century AD. We shall disregard the fact that The Peshitta has only 22 of the 27 books that make up the version I have tested with Codefinder, in which all these long codes occur. We shall also ignore the fact that John 7:53 to 8:11 is missing in all Peshitta mss. but is found in the Codefinder edition (from The Palestinian Syriac edition). Luke 22:17,18 are also missing from The Peshitta but found in The Codefinder edition. The Codefinder edition is essentially the 1905 Syriac New Testament originally published by The British Bible Society which has also been republished in The 1979 United Bible Society of The Syriac Bible. Other editions also include these and the other mentioned verses and books. If a translator were responsible for these codes, he would have had to do the entire translation of all 27 books himself (from Greek, presumably , compose and keep track of every code and code letter of all codes and skip rates of 17,921, 18,474 ,-35,348,70,328,74,806 ,to 99,067 simultaneously, while translating the Greek accurately . The 61 letter code of skip -35,348 reads backwards in Aramaic ! The first letter starts at Hebrews 7:19. letter 9 & goes backward 18 chapters to locate the second letter in Colossians 1:6; the twelfth letter lands at Matthew 18:14 , the thirteenth lands back in Revelation 21:6 . The code continues to go backward through the NT a total of 4.6 times and ends at Luke 20:33.letter 14.
The last code I have displayed is a string of 98 letters found at a skip 74,806 and going through the Aramaic New Testament 15.74 times. It starts at Ephesians Ch 1 V 16 Letter 35 and ends at Acts Ch 20 V 15 Letter 35. What is really interesting is that this 98 letter string doubles as a Hebrew code and also as an Aramaic code. The Hebrew code has 93 letters and The Aramaic code uses 77 of the same 98 letter string. One 29 letter Aramaic

code , when read backward , reveals a 23 letter Hebrew code. All these fit into a story line of the last day of Christ's life , His death, resurrection, ascension and session over the church afterward.

Could a human translator have devised and coordinated all this ? I don't see how one could devise one of the six long codes listed, much less all of them, going through the NT up to 16 times each, spaced 9 to 45 chapters between each code letter, reading forward and backwards, in Hebrew and Aramaic languages, all about the Messiah's birth, suffering,death, resurrection,ascension and kingdom in Heaven. Even if a super computer were available 1500 years ago, such a feat would have been impossible. I challenge anyone today to construct a text of NT size and with one such long code running through its 350 pages.

If a translator had been able to do so, what reason would he have for doing it? Who would have been able to detect it ? (I also assume it would be more difficult to compose such a code than it would be to detect it) . Remember, it had to accurately reflect the Greek text it supposedly translated.

I contend that these codes effectively dispose of the translation theory of The Peshitta NT. The codes cannot be explained if <u>The Peshitta NT</u> is a translation. One must understand that there is no ancient ms. containing all NT books. That is simply not how The NT was written or translated. Each book was written individually or translated individually. The Peshitta mss. are written on animal skins;the modern book style, or codex, was invented in the third century; scrolls were used before that, but regardless the format, even if The Peshitta were a translation, there are no whole New Testament manuscripts among the most ancient Peshitta mss. .The Peshitta was hardly written in one volume, therefore it would be highly unlikely on that basis alone, that there were codes written by a human writer. There is no evidence that it was written all together as a unified whole NT.

A second possible explanation for these codes is that the original NT text was Aramaic and that the seven authors conspired together to write all the books together fairly quickly with all the codes incorporated in the original , coordinated in each of the twenty seven books in their present order (which in the Eastern versions is different from the Western book order). This scenario would be more difficult to defend than the first one, as I see it. Revelation was written from the Isle of Patmos by John The Apostle. It is absurd to think all the other books were written there at the same time by all seven men. We know Paul wrote five epistles from prison in Rome at various times. The Gospels and the General Epistles were not written from Paul's prison cell. If the NT books were all written at the same time and place, then they are false testimonies and not to be accepted as scripture at all, for some of them give different places of origin.

The original NT books were certainly written by different men in different places at different times, over a period of at least thirty years. It is most unlikely that they all had seen each other at any time, much less at the same time. Seven men would have a much more difficult time coordinating such code writing than one man, as each would have to follow and pick up where another left off, counting the letter sequences as they occur in the previous (or following) book. The whole idea is unwieldy and bizarre, for we cannot imagine why or how anyone would attempt such a thing as this. No one would have been able to detect these codes at the time they were written. A computer would have been required, and that was 1900 years off.

The only explanation that makes sense is that God Himself authored This Aramaic New Testament and put the codes in it for our generation to discover. The text was to be reconstructed as originally written, which was not difficult, since there are few significant differences among Peshitta mss. .Because they were so carefully copied, all that is needed is to compare mss. and follow the majority reading where there are differences. I will not get into the details of textual criticism here;suffice it to say that the Divine authorship of this 27 book AramaicNew Testament is by far the best explanation for the codes; As I see it, it is the only explanation.

Divine Contact-The Original New Testament Discovered

Of course it is possible that these long codes are not designed at all, but are simply the product of chance. The probability of this is extremely small, on the order of 10^{-460}, **or one in 10** to the 460th power (1 with 460 zeroes after it). The number ELS's calculation and the chance calculation for each ELS ("code" word) is a very accurate formula.DNA evidence comes nowhere close to this order of probability. If this is not proof, there is no such thing as proof !

God has preserved His words perfectly for thousands of years and will call the world of unbelievers and atheists to consider the evidence in His word, including the codes, that show there is a God Who alone could have put such long codes (191 letters) in a 2000 year old text, each letter of which is separated by 74,806 letters of text (more than the length of the Gospel of Luke) , in two ancient languages, Hebrew and Aramaic, the languages in which The Bible was written, using the same code letters for codes in both languages, in both forward and reverse coding , throughout the NT books, which books were written by many different authors at different times in different locations, yet each code exists as if the entire NT were written by one person at one time with a letter of code in Matthew, and the next 74,806 letters away in Mark, then again 74,806 letters away in Luke, etc. , 97 times altogether , going through the NT 15 times. What human being could do that today with a super computer ! What Extra Terrestrial (assuming the existence of ET's) could have done it in the first century ? He would have had to arrange the writing of 27 books over a period of years by different writers , letter by letter, coordinating the numbers of letters and arrangement of letters just as they are in the Peshitta edition I used in Codefinder, (which is based on mss. hand copied by scribes of both Eastern Assyrian and Western Syrian churches. The Eastern Peshitta does not contain 2nd Peter, 2nd & 3rd John, Jude or Revelation . The Western text has those books , but the edition with the codes follows Eastern mss. in certain Gospels. The book of Revelation has a text that is unique to one manuscript, not traditionally used by any church. It is part of the modern edition of The Syriac NT.

And if an ET could pull off something like the above , whose existence I do not concede, why in the name of Sam Hill would he ? Why write a New Testament about a Messiah Son of God , called Jehovah, Who is born in Bethlehem and dies on a cross in Jerusalem for the salvation of the world ?
The codes I have found would not exist if one letter were added to The Peshitta NT edition I have used ! This particular edition did not exist (as far as I can tell) until December of AD 2000. If one letter were deleted, the codes would not exist !

What ! Did an ET put the codes in 27 individual books 2000 years ago and then wait 2000 years to cause someone to put together **just the right mss. readings into one edition, with the books arranged in the Eastern church order** (Matthew,Mark,Luke,John,Acts,James,1 Peter,2 Peter,1 John, 2 John,3 John,Jude, Romans, 1 & Cor. , etc. through Hebrews, then Revelation)? Such control over men, down to the letter arrangement of 27 books written by at least seven different men in different places at different times and then coordinating events 2000 years later to bring together each ms. with the exact wording of the original- such control and intelligence is to make an ET the Supreme Being and all of us subjects to it-him-her-them. In other words, an atheist making such an argument would not really be an atheist; he would be worshipping an ET, investing it with all the Divine attributes of omniscience, omnipotence and omnipresence , as God ! That would be an incredibly stupid proposition to offer in an attempt to avoid the God hypothesis, since he would be making ET into God.

The fact is , the God hypothesis is unavoidable in explaining the Peshitta codes.

Apparently God put the codes in The Peshitta to be discovered in this century when computers and software were developed that could find them. The only software capable of finding these toroidal codes (codes found by making the text an endless loop) is Codefinder , as far as I can tell. It is also the only program with which to search The Peshitta NT. No other software package has it.

There is very little wiggle room whereby an atheist might escape from the facts present here. God is the only explanation . **This is scientific evidence proving The New Testament is authored by God , The Father of Jesus Christ, through His Holy Spirit. An overstatement ? Not if you consider the extensive data I have compiled by an ongoing experiment to search for 95 Divine Names and Titles as codes in The same Peshitta text.** The experiment tests for the numbers of such ELS's. Each Name should occur a certain number of times by skipping letters . Each is a relatively short word of 2 to 7 letters. Each Name can be predicted to have a certain expected number of occurrences statistically with a very accurate formula , based on text size and letter frequencies. A non coded text produces entirely predictable results. Each search of The Peshitta is compared with a control text which is a scrambled Peshitta text of the same size and letter frequencies as The Peshitta. The control text shows entirely predictable results.

The Peshitta does not- not by a long shot ! The Names and Titles of God in Hebrew and Aramaic , as found written in Hebrew Old and Aramaic New Testaments occur in highly significant numbers throughout The Peshitta NT.

The cumulative results for that experiment yield a probability for the 367 searches of 95 Divine Names of 1 in 10^{2100} .

The evidence demands that God put the codes in The Peshitta NT , and that it was not a generic God, or a pagan god, but The God revealed in The Bible, Whose very names and Titles are revealed there, as well as His nature and deeds. He has endorsed The Old and New Testaments by such codes, as they are found throughout both, in Hebrew and Aramaic texts. I do believe The Hebrew Bible needs a bit more editing to bring it to its original condition. Such editing may be done on the basis of the Massora preserved for many 20 + centuries , in which the scribes kept notes of changes made in the text – for instance, there are 134 places where "**Yahweh**" was changed to "**Adonai**" in the text. Those places are all noted in the Massora. Other such changes were made as well. If these are corrected, I predict more codes will be found in The Hebrew Tanach and many will parallel those of The Peshitta in skip range and text coverage, going through the entire Tanach text for each code finding.

Oh , I know this sounds too good to be true to some. To those I say, "Prove me wrong". Find such codes as I show here in another text. Make sure they are long and valid grammatically. They would have to occur in a text of similar size to The NT and be at least 25 letters long. They would have to make some semblance of sense. As far as I can tell, the skeptics and naysayers have yet to meet those conditions. Until they do, I maintain my hypothesis that God wrote The Peshitta NT and coded it with information about Himself , His Son and The Holy Spirit, with His Names and Titles encoded hundreds of thousands of times more than expected as a Divine signature and fingerprint, validating the text as His work.

It is the job of a scientist to formulate an hypothesis, test the hypothesis by an experiment, gather and analyze the data, evaluate the hypothesis in light of the data and state conclusions. He or she must then set out, not to prove, but to disprove the hypothesis. In this, the skeptics serve to accomplish the hard work of testing the hypothesis. Most proponents of an idea try simply to support that idea, whereas the opponents will attack it and put it to the reality test. The enemies of an idea do it the greatest service. They will throw reality at it until it either falls apart or proves impregnable. I hope to test this hypothesis by continuing to search other texts for such codes.

I have verified that The Peshitta NT is the original NT from which The Greek NT was translated, by ten additional methods of analysis. These I have displayed on my web site , http://AramaicNT.com . I have also included them in my book , <u>Divine Contact</u>. These then lend secondary support to the main hypothesis that God wrote The Peshitta NT and encoded it, since that would also assume that The Peshitta is the original NT and not a translation.

If this proves to be what I think it is, this discovery will shake and change the world for good . Science and Religion will never be the same as a result. I leave it to the reader to imagine the implications and repercussions possible.

תשבוחתא למשיחא במרומא
Tishbokhta l'Meshikha b'mruma
Glory to The Messiah in the highest !

To my knowledge, these long codes I have found in The Peshitta are ground-breaking discoveries, being the first long codes found in The New Testament. They two things:

1. The Aramaic Peshitta New Testament was not composed by human intelligence; it must have come from a much greater intellect.(I have found over 80 of God's names coded millions of times more than are expected by chance throughout The entire NT. The effect does not occur in other texts.)
2. The Aramaic Peshitta-Peshitto NT is the original New Testament, contrary to the conventional teaching that The Greek NT is the original.The Greek is a translation of The Aramaic, not vice-versa.

The experiment I have performed on The Peshitta and on control texts reveals an incredible phenomenon which could only have been revealed to the world in our time when the computer was invented and developed , so that we could analyze the text of the Bible in ways before impossible.

תשבוחתא לאלהא במרומא ועל ארעא שלמא וסברא טבא לבני אנשא
Glory to God in the highest, and on earth peace, good news to the children of men -Luke 2:14.

Both long codes in The Peshitta say something about this Aramaic New Testament. Add one letter to or delete one letter from Matthew and both codes disappear. Add one letter to or delete one letter from the rest of it (aside from 1st Peter) and the second code disappears.

Does this mean that The Peshitta is the perfect replica of the original NEW TESTAMENT ? I would like to believe that , but I don't think that is the logical conclusion to the above line of reasoning. What it may mean is that The Peshitta as it exists today (and the Eastern Church of Syria claims The Peshitta is unchanged from the 1st century, see history of Peshitta above) is exactly the text God chose to encode with these messages.

I have found much more convincing evidence to support this position by discovering thousands, even millions of a different type of code in The Peshitta. Ed Sherman introduced this concept in his "Bible Code Digest' and referred to what he called, "Bible mosaics". He found that short 2 to 5 letter names in Genesis occurred in highly unusual numbers as codes at many skip sequences in Gen. 1 – 17. These occurrences are subject to statistical analysis, which gives *extremely low probabilities* for the occurrences of these words.

> I have been so impressed with what I have found in The Peshitta that I determined to learn Aramaic and to translate the entire Peshitta New Testament into English in an interlinear (word for word, literal translation). As I translate , I find that walking into The Peshitta is like walking through the wardrobe in C.S. Lewis' Chronicles of Narnia, (now a blockbuster movie). It takes you into another land altogether.
> It really is a magical experience; a doorway into pure truth
> - the kingdom of the spirit--of The Voice-of Him.
> Here, everything is **clear**; everything is **sure**; everything is **absolute**; everything is **forever**.

> I hope and pray the world will be able to get a glimpse of that, as people read <u>The Aramaic-English Interlinear Gospels</u>, published by myself, January, 2006, and then the rest of The New Testament when I release it ,hopefully, later this year.

I reproduce here part of my prologue:

Even if The Peshitta were a translation, or any of the Aramaic NT books were translations, the text as it exits in the edition I have, did not exist in any Peshitta scroll or codex in the fifth century or earlier. Many books exist in single book manuscripts or sections of the NT. Gospels are usually separate from Epistles. Western Peshitta mss. do not have Revelation or five of The General Epistles in the same text as the Critical edition in The Syriac NT.

No translator(s) could have pulled off a feat like what I have described, even with a super computer and super advanced software. I seriously doubt we will ever be able to invent such codes hidden in a text by spacing the letters so far apart , connecting the text end to beginning, and make several sentences or paragraphs in each one, all grammatically correct and coherent, each telling a related Gospel message about The Messiah, God and The Holy Spirit, The Birth, Suffering, Death and Resurrection of Yeshua Meshikha, each in beautiful **Aramaic** or **Hebrew** poetry !

It appears to me that God put these codes in the Aramaic New Testament to be discovered in the computer age, when many are skeptical and without faith in God or The Bible, but have faith in technology. There were no computers when The New Testament was written, yet computer technology is required to find these codes I have found in The New Testament. *Since no mere human, reading or studying the text, could have found these codes without a computer, I affirm that no mere human in the first century or in any century before the computer age could have put them there*; nor would he have reason to. It would seem that the human difficulty of composing these codes would far exceed the difficulty of finding them. If the seven long codes are not proof enough, I have found millions of Divine Name codes in the NT, via an experiment, far beyond statistical chance occurrence numbers, that pinpoint The Codemaker's identity.

I further affirm that this discovery demonstrates at least eight truths:

1. The God and Christ of God of <u>The New Testament</u> exist and are exactly Who and What that New Testament says they are.
2. The New Testament in which these scientific proofs exist is absolutely true in all its statements, i.e.- **infallible**- historically, theologically, prophetically, scientifically, grammatically, geographically and textually-where it presents data concerning what pertains to the claimed statements and activities of God, Christ and The Holy Spirit. Whatever statements or actions are attributed to humans , angels or demons are also accurately recorded and are true history, though , unlike Divine statements, may not be necessarily true statements, since human and diabolical errors and lies are also accurately recorded.
3. The original New Testament was written in Aramaic and has been preserved to this day with 100% word accuracy in The 27 books of The Peshitta-Peshitto form I have tested, and in which I have found volumes of coded information.
4. Greek is not the original language in which any New Testament book was written.
5. The Greek New Testament is a translation of the original Aramaic text in all 27 books of the Western New Testament canon.
6. The number of letters in The original New Testament was and is **461,094**. It is possible that the completed text as written approx. 1950 years ago had some few spelling differences in a few places or compound word division differences, but the total number of letters was the same.

7   God and His Son love you eternally, and have provided for your eternal welfare and joy.

8   Nothing can separate you from that love.

(will pass away) נעברון (& the Earth) וארעא (Heaven) שמיא
(will pass away) נעברן (not) לא (& My words) ומלי

-Matthew 24:35(Bauscher's Peshitta Interlinear)

"Heaven and Earth will pass away and My words will not pass away."
- Our Lord Jesus Christ (Maran Yeshua Meshikha)

High Tech. section (Chapters 12-16) -The Science of the Codes

Chapter 12- The Peshitta Codes Experiment

The following material is technical in nature as it abounds with experimental data and statistical and linguistic analysis.

(The entire 50 page data table for this experiment is viewable at my web site:http://aramaicnt.com)

Based on my long code findings shown above, I devised a scientific experiment to test the following hypothesis:

If God were to put codes in the Bible, he would leave a signature in it using the names and titles of God which are mentioned in the plain Bible text, and insure that they occur in highly significant numbers, *far beyond or below statistically expected amounts. These would constitute a divine signature of the author of the books individually, the separate testaments and the Bible as a whole.*

The control texts should not produce significant results.

The following is an article I had published in *Bible Code Digest,* **an online periodical dedicated to**

research in Bible codes, hosted by Ed Sherman, a professional Mathematician and Statistician.

Contact: Aramaic New Testament Codes Revealed

*Researcher Claims Breakthrough Discovery
in the Aramaic Version, Written in the Language of Jesus*

By Rev. Glenn David Bauscher

My Hypothesis: If God were to put codes in the Bible, He would certainly leave a signature in it using the names and titles of God which are mentioned in the plain Bible text, and insure that they occur in highly significant numbers, far beyond or below statistically expected amounts. These would constitute a divine signature of the Author of the books individually, the separate testaments and the Bible as a whole.

Based on my previous long code findings in the Peshitta New Testament (The Aramaic New Testament, written in the tongue which Jesus and his countrymen of 1st century Israel spoke), I completed the results of a long series of comparisons of results from the Peshitta and control texts.

The Comparisons

After Ed Sherman (Bible Code Digest director) introduced the Bible code Mosaics concept from Genesis, I experimented in that and other books. I analyzed the results statistically to see if there are patterns and low probabilities, using chi-square analysis and standard deviation calculations. I started with two letter names and titles, gradually including three, then four and five letter names and titles. I have found highly significant results in all the Old Testament books that I have searched using the names of God, including Genesis, Exodus, Leviticus, Esther and 2nd Chronicles. Control texts, such as Tolstoy's War and Peace in Hebrew, and other texts, have not yielded similar results.

I applied this method to the Peshitta and modified it, searching for the titles of God, His Son and the Holy Spirit. I have not returned empty handed. The results are staggering!

I am still overwhelmed by all of this, because it seems that no matter which New Testament book I search or which of the considerable number of divine titles I enter into Codefinder, the search software I used for these comparisons, the probability for the actual number of occurrences compared to the expected occurrences is infinitesimal. I have also used control texts with which to compare each Bible finding. Control texts like War and Peace in Hebrew show nothing like the results I find in **the Peshitta NT**. In other words, **the Peshitta NT** contains highly significant numbers of divine names and titles compared to what is expected by chance.

These divine names are the signature codes to which I referred at the beginning of this chapter and elsewhere. It is similar to the long series of prime numbers received from space, in the movie Contact, starring Jodie Foster. Not only do they indicate an intelligent author for the individual books of the Bible, but they also indicate a single superhuman intelligence as the author of the entire New Testament as a single unified whole.

Presentation of Sample Results

In the first table we have a comparison between the variations from the expected number of occurrences of Yahweh as an ELS in the Peshitta text and in a control text (a scrambled version of the Peshitta).

Yahweh (יהוה) in the New Testament

Skip Range*	Variation from Expected		%-age Variation	
	Control	Peshitta	Control	Peshitta
1,000 to 50,000	1,046	22,524	0.2%	4.3%
-1,000 to -50,000	936	30,230	0.2%	5.7%
50,001 to 153,633	2,831	41,793	0.6%	9.3%
-50,001 to -153,633	2,399	3,142	0.5%	0.7%

*There are 527,456 expected occurrences for each of the first two skip range categories, and 451,461 for the last two categories

As an example, let's look at the results for ELSs with skips in the range of 1,000 up to 50,000. Yahweh is expected to appear as an ELS 527,456 times in both the Peshitta and the control text. And yet the actual number of occurrences of the Yahweh ELS differ from the expected number by 22,524 in the Peshitta while only differing by 1,046 in the control text. So the size of the variation in the

Peshitta is 21.5 times greater than that in the control text. While the variation was only 0.2% from expected in the control text, it was 4.3% in the Peshitta. The size of the variation for the control text is well within what would be expected on the basis of random phenomena. The Peshitta variations, however, are far greater than that for all but the fourth skip size category.

The next table presents comparable results for occurrences of the Mariah ELS. Mariah is the Aramaic equivalent of Yahweh.

Mariah (מריא) in the New Testament

Skip Range*	Variation from Expected		%-age Variation	
	Control	Peshitta	Control	Peshitta
1,000 to 50,000	1,670	123	0.3%	0.0%
-1,000 to -50,000	2,858	15,904	0.4%	2.4%
50,001 to 153,633	3,288	19,341	0.6%	3.4%
-50,001 to -153,633	534	66,109	0.1%	11.7%

*There are 658,442 expected occurrences for each of the first two skip range categories, and 563,554 for the last two categories.

While the size of the variations in the control text are all within the range of what would be expected due to chance, the variations for all but the first skip size category are far greater than anything due to chance.

The next table presents comparable results for occurrences of the Alaha ELS. Alaha is the Aramaic equivalent of Elohim, another Hebrew name for God.

Alaha (אלהא) in the New Testament

Skip Range*	Variation from Expected		%-age Variation	
	Control	Peshitta	Control	Peshitta
1,000 to 50,000	1,533	24,282	0.1%	1.6%
-1,000 to -50,000	3,326	40,040	0.2%	2.7%
50,001 to 153,633	15,690	8,824	1.2%	0.7%
-50,001 to -153,633	12,409	126,743	1.0%	9.8%

*There are 1,508,834 expected occurrences for each of the first two skip range categories, and 1,291,420 for the last two categories.

Again we see that the size of the variations in the control text are all within the range of what would be expected due to chance, while the variations for the second and fourth skip size categories are far greater than anything due to chance.

If we add up the variations from expected for each skip size category by divine name, we have the following comparison.

	Total Variation		Ratio of Peshitta to Control
ELSs	Control	Peshitta	
Yahweh	7,212	**97,689**	**13.5**
Mariah	8,350	**101,477**	**12.2**
Alaha	32,958	**199,889**	**6.1**
Total of Above	48,520	**399,055**	**8.2**

Comparison of Total Variations from Expected in the Peshitta and the Control Text

As we can see, the total amount of variation from expected in the Peshitta ranges from six times to 13.5 times more than the total variation from expected in the control text—for the different divine names. This is an extremely significant result statistically because the sample sizes are exceptionally large (i.e., 400,000 or more in each category).

To summarize, the graph below presents the above comparisons in terms of Z-values (the size of the variation in terms of standard deviations). Ordinarily, differences from expected almost always are less than 4 standard deviations (defined as the square root of the expected number of occurrences). However, some of the variations from expected for the control texts are greater than 4. This is due to the fact that variations from expected for a given ELS at one skip size tend to be similar to those for adjacent skip sizes. For example, if the Yahweh ELS appears 20% more often than expected with skips of 1,000, it will also tend to appear much more often than expected with skips of 999 and 1,001. That the Yahweh ELS appeared 20% more often than expected with a skip of 1,000 was probably due, at least in part, to segments of the text where the letter frequencies of the letters in Yahweh were greater than average. When that occurs, it will also tend to cause the Yahweh ELS to appear much more often for skips slightly greater or smaller than 1,000.

Because of the sensitivity of variations from expected to differences in letter frequencies in different parts of a text, the size of the variations from expected in the control text can be as great as 15 standard deviations, rather than just 4.

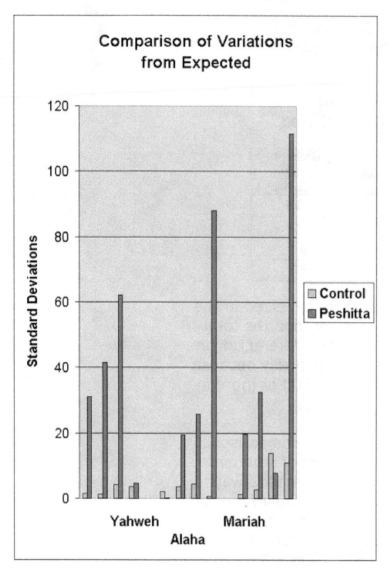

If variations due to chance should almost never be greater than 15 standard deviations, how then can we explain many of the variations noted above that are far greater than that? The largest variations are 111.5, 88.1, 62.2, 41.6, 32.6 and 31.1 standard deviations from expected. Variations of these magnitudes basically eliminate chance as an explanation.

A Comparison From the Torah

What would the above types of comparisons look like if we examined occurrences of the Yahweh ELS in the Torah—versus a control text of comparable length from a Hebrew version of Tolstoy's War and Peace? That comparison is provided in the next table.

Yahweh (יהוה) in the Torah
(With War & Peace as a Control)

Skip Range*	Variation from Expected		%-age Variation	
	Control	Torah	Control	Torah
10 to 101,250	6,169	36,826	0.3%	2.7%
-10 to -101,250	2,196	62,124	0.1%	4.6%
Total of Above	8,365	98,950	0.2%	3.6%

*There are 2,071,362 expected occurrences in the War & Peace control text and 1,358,276 expected occurrences in the Torah.

Again, we see that the size of the variations is radically higher in the Torah than in the War & Peace control text.

Conclusions

While there are major difficulties in accurately determining the probability that any or all of the above dramatic variations exhibited in the Peshitta text and the Torah were due to chance, no matter what method is used to estimate that probability, the result is conclusive—such enormous variations cannot be due to chance.

The effects described above are not only observable in the whole New Testament, but also in the individual Gospels, the book of Acts, the book of Hebrews and the Revelation, as well as the first twelve chapters of Matthew as a separate section. The individual books overall would generally need to exhibit the same traits in order for the entire New Testament to contain such significant and unusual numbers of ELS's (equidistant letter sequences), compared to the expected numbers for the entire New Testament! (Note: Recent testing of additional epistles show the same effect in Acts, Titus, Romans, 1st and 2nd Corinthians and even Philemon, which is only one page.)

The results of the comparisons presented above are very compelling evidence to support the assertion that the Peshitta-Peshitto New Testament is the original and divinely-inspired text of the apostles.

Divine Contact-The Original New Testament Discovered

To those who are conversant in New Testament textual criticism, I know all this may sound fanciful. The ruling school of thought is that the Peshitta is simply a retranslation of the traditional (revised) Greek text in the early 5th century. But it is my personal belief that we need a fresh look at all that is considered sacrosanct in the field of New Testament textual criticism. Much of it is mere conjecture. There is no historical evidence for either a Syrian revision or a Greek revision in that time period.

Something as drastic as changing, overnight, the sacred text of the Bible which had been accepted for centuries, is not likely to occur without a prolonged resistance and struggle, and even then will most likely only be received by some, not all. However, it is stretching credulity beyond the breaking point to affirm that two such revisions occurred (Syrian and Greek), replacing all other Aramaic and Greek texts in all Syrian and Greek churches, without one word of mention by any of the church fathers, historians, or anyone at all. There is no council, edict, or order such as one finds when church doctrine (Council of Nicaea) was debated or the canon of the Bible was settled (Council of Carthage).

To reiterate my original hypothesis: If God were to put codes in the Bible, He would certainly leave a signature in it using the names and titles of God which are mentioned in the plain Bible text, and insure that they occur in highly significant numbers, far beyond or below statistically expected amounts. These would constitute a divine signature of the Author of the books individually, the separate testaments and the bible as a whole.

I conclude that the data support the hypothesis overwhelmingly. My comparisons apply specifically to the Jacobite Peshitto New Testament. It appears that this text has the divine signature all through its 27 individual books and the work as a whole, having extreme variations in the actual numbers of divine names, as compared to expected values and the control results in War and Peace.

This investigation will continue. I welcome others to join in it. I am impressed with an overwhelming sense of awe.

"My heart standeth in awe of thy word." - Psalm 119:161

I believe the heavens have made contact.

What is the Peshitta?

There are two ancient versions of the Peshitta, the New Testament in Aramaic; one is used by the Assyrian Nestorians and the other, called the Peshitto, is used by the Syrian Monophysites—also called Jacobites.

These groups were formed by a split in the Eastern Church concerning which occurred in A.D. 451. Both—the doctrine of who Christ is—Christology groups had used the same Aramaic Bible and have continued to hold fast to it, even to this day. Neither group would have held to a text which the other produced, so it is in vain to suggest that either side produced or revised the text at that or a later time.

Another distinctive feature of both these versions, which helps to more precisely date them, is the fact that each originally excluded (the Eastern Church does still) 2 Peter, 2 John, 3 John, Jude and Revelation. This is a testament to the fact that the Peshitta-Peshitto was formed before the Council of Carthage in AD 397, when the canon of scripture became official and standard. Apparently, the Eastern Churches received their New Testament at a very early stage of its formation, even before the canon included John's Revelation, the last book to be written, circa A.D. 95. It would seem they took the New Testament "hot off the press."

Variations

There are very few and slight variations in the two versions. I have copies of both versions and have compared them. Results are below.

Remember that the Eastern Church has always insisted that its New Testament is unchanged from the apostles' time unto the present.

—The Gospel of Mark in both versions has one significant spelling or word variation per page.The same applies to Matthew.
—In Luke, the Peshitto and the Peshitta versions differ even less than in Matthew and Mark.
—In John, compensating for the exclusion of chapter 7:53-8:11 from the Nestorian text and its inclusion in the Jacobite version, the two versions differ about the same as in Luke.
—The book of Galatians in the Jacobite Peshitto varies in about one word or letter per page from the Nestorian Peshitta.

I have been unable to compare more than these five books thus far.

Divine Contact-The Original New Testament Discovered

These are counts based on Stephen Silver's collation of The Eastern Khaburis manuscript with The 1905 Syriac Peshitto of United Bible Society. They are incredible statistics in themselves, considering that these texts must be at least 1600 years old.

The text that I used for analysis of codes throughout is the Jacobite text. Both texts now include the formerly missing Revelation, 2 Peter, 2 and 3 John and Jude. The ancient manuscripts of the Peshitta extant today include a considerable number of 5th and 6th century documents.

If there is any New Testament text which answers to the Hebrew Old Testament text for carefulness and faithfulness of preservation as well as consistency among its approx. 350 manuscripts, that New Testament text is the Peshitta-Peshitto. Moreover, Aramaic has the best claim for being the original language of the New Testament. Historical evidence (Josephus) and internal evidence ("to the Jew first", "beginning at Jerusalem, in Judea," etc.) are decidedly in favor of an original Aramaic New Testament which was translated into Greek, rather than vice-versa.

Scholars have generally agreed that The Peshitta and Peshitto Bibles are in very close agreement with the Traditional Received Text of the New Testament (and Old Testament, for that matter). No other text type is closer to it than the Majority Greek Text, also known as the Textus Receptus, for most of the New Testament. The Peshitta is the earliest witness for the Majority text type, which was the foundation of The King James Version of the Bible, first published in 1611.

My comparisons of The Peshitta and The Majority Text in the Gospels show 75% agreement between these two when The Critical Text (the text used by NIV, Living Bible, New American Standard Version and most other modern translations) differs from the Majority.

The Old Testament portion is probably a first century translation of the Hebrew Bible by Christian translators, making it the second oldest translation and complete witness to the Hebrew Bible (and the oldest *Semitic* witness), the Greek Septuagint being the oldest.

In Jan. 2003 the following article appeared in Bible Code Digest:
Massive Jesus Mosaic Pervades the Aramaic New Testament

An enormous mathematical variation, or mosaic, has been discovered in appearances of Jesus (Yeshu) ELSs in the

Divine Contact-The Original New Testament Discovered

Peshitta, or Aramaic New Testament. These variations could not possibly have occurred by chance, and analysis shows that they were intentionally encoded, even though the text was authored by several writers over a number of years.

Researcher Rev. Glenn David Bauscher discovered the patterns formed by occurrences of Jesus with skips greater than 50,000 in the Aramaic New Testament. We reported earlier on other initial results from his research in the <u>October issue.</u>

In the first table we have a comparison between the variations from the expected number of occurrences of Yeshu (Jesus) as an ELS in the Peshitta text and in a control text (a scrambled version of the Peshitta).

Yeshu (ישו) in the New Testament

Skip Range*	Variation from Expected		%-age Variation	
	Control	Peshitta	Control	Peshitta
100 to 50,000	4,813	130	-0.1%	0.0%
-100 to -50,000	13,940	12,630	0.3%	0.3%
50,001 to 230,500	29,409	520,240	0.3%	6.2%
-50,001 to -230,500	122,889	227,060	1.5%	2.7%

*There are 5,292,161 expected occurrences for each of the first two skip range categories, and 8,411,016 for the last two categories.

While the results for the first two skip range categories are very comparable, and uninteresting, those for ELSs with skips greater than 50,000 are radically different. The actual number of occurrences of the Yeshu ELS in these higher ranges differs from the expected number by 520,240 in the Peshitta while only differing by 29,409 in the control text. So the size of the variation in the Peshitta is 17.7 times greater than that in the control text. While the variation was only 0.3% from expected in the control text, it was 6.2% in the Peshitta. The size of the variation for the control text is well within what would be expected on the basis of random phenomena. The Peshitta variations, however, are decidedly greater than that for the last two skip size categories.

The following graph provides a side-by-side comparison of the variations from expected for a more detailed breakdown of skip size ranges. It is evident that the mosaic effect for Yeshu ELSs in the Peshitta is exceptionally strong. In this way, Bible codes consisting of the short form of the name of Jesus affirm the supernatural authorship of the Aramaic New Testament.

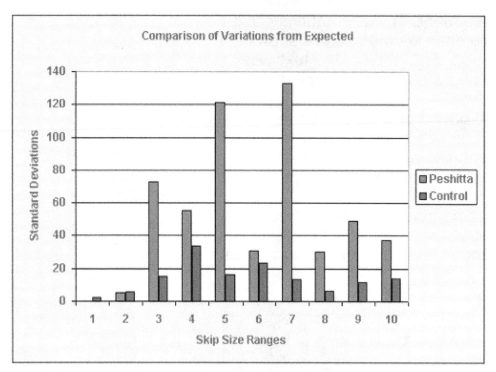

The following table provides a key to the definitions of the numbered skip size ranges in the above graph.

Skip Size Range Number	Skip Sizes
1	100 to 50,000
2	-100 to -50,000
3	50,001 to 100,000
4	-50,001 to -100,000
5	100,001 to 140,000
6	-100,001 to -140,000
7	140,001 to 170,000
8	-140,001 to -170,000
9	170,001 to 230,500
10	-170,001 to -230,500

Because of the sensitivity of variations from expected to differences in letter frequencies in different parts of a text, the size of the variations from expected in the control text can be as great as 25 standard deviations, rather than just 4.

If variations due to chance should almost never be greater than 25 standard deviations, how then can we explain many of the variations noted above that are far greater than that? The largest variations are 133, 121, 73, 55 and 49 standard deviations from expected. Variations of these magnitudes are far greater than those that could be due to chance.

In January 2005, Bible Code Digest published the following :

The Controversy Over Mosaics: Round Five
Given a Hebrew word, a search text and a range of skip sizes, leading code software will instantly tell you how many times ELSs of that word will appear—by chance. What are we to make of instances where there is a large difference between the expected number of occurrences and the number of times the given ELS actually appears? And what if large differences occur for many different skip size ranges? When that happens, we call it a "mosaic."

Now, we aren't talking about an ELS that is only expected to appear one or two times in the search text. We're talking about ELSs that are expected to appear 50 or 500 or 5,000 times—because the ELS only consists of a few letters.

Let's look at an interesting example. Take the Hebrew word Eckad (alef-khet-dalet), which means "one." It is undoubtedly one of the most significant words in the Jewish faith. It appears at the end of the Shema of Deuteronomy 6:4 ("Shema Yisrael! Adonai Elohenu Adonai Eckad" or "Hear O Israel! The Lord is our God, the Lord is one."). This places it at the heart of Judaism and its belief in a single, living God. Within the first 17 chapters of Genesis, the three-letter-long Eckad ELS consistently appears much more often than expected by chance over all but one range of skip sizes, as shown in the following table.

The Eckad Mosaic in Genesis 1-17

Smallest Skip Size	Largest Skip Size	Expected Number of Occurrences	Excess Number of Occurrences	Percentage Deviation from Expected
2	1,000	2,195	146	+6.6%
1,001	2,000	1,972	196	+9.9%
2,001	3,000	1,746	183	+10.5%
3,001	4,000	1,521	307	+20.2%
4,001	5,000	1,295	313	+24.2%
5,001	6,000	1,069	326	+30.4%
6,001	7,000	844	408	+48.4%
7,001	8,000	618	255	+41.3%
8,001	9,000	392	101	+25.7%
9,001	10,238	173	-7	-4.1%
2	10,238	11,829	2,234	18.9%

For example, the Eckad ELS appears 1,252 times with skips between 6,001 and 7,000 within Genesis 1-17, even though it is only expected to appear 844 times. That it should appear 48.4% more often than expected by chance seems highly unlikely.

The following graph summarizes the above results.

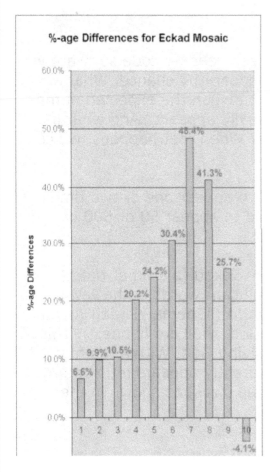

Mosaics differ from traditional ELS findings in a number of key ways. First, for mosaics, the shorter the ELS, the better; while for traditional ELSs, the longer the ELS, the better. Second, a broad range of skip sizes is included in a mosaic; whereas, for traditional ELSs, typically the focus is only on the occurrence with the shortest skip, or those with the shortest skips.

The phenomenon of mosaics has been covered in seven past issues of BCD. These issues cover key parts of the introduction and debate over the potential reality of this kind of Bible code phenomena. (To view Digests prior to January 2002, click on Subscribers and log on with your user name and password. Then, scroll to the bottom of the page and select the Digest you would like to view. We have provided links in the text below for Digests after January 2002.)

In the November and December 2000 issues, BCD introduced the concept, much as was done above. Questions were raised by skeptics, who asserted that mosaics are simply caused by dramatic differences in letter frequencies between various parts of the search text.

What was the problem? Take the Eckad mosaic, for example, and let us assume that Genesis 1-17 is 20,000 letters long (it is actually slightly longer). Within that search text, the Eckad ELS with the longest possible skip would be one where the letters were the 1st, the 10,000th and the 19,999th. Now consider all Eckad ELSs with skips of 9,000 to 9,999. The first possible such ELS would cover letters 1, 9,001 and 18,001 and the last possible such ELS would cover letters 2,000, 11,000 and 20,000. Thus, all of the letters of the Eckad ELSs in this skip size range appear in three ranges: 1-2,000, 9,001-11,000 and 18,001-20,000.

First Letter Number	Last Letter Number	Potential Letters in an Eckad ELS with a Skip of 9,000-9,999?
1	2,000	Yes
2,001	9,000	No
9,001	11,000	Yes
11,001	18,000	No
18,001	20,000	Yes

Given this, none of the Eckad ELSs with skips in this size range would include any letters in the ranges of 2,001-9,000 and 11,001-18,000. This would mean that none of the Eckad ELSs would draw from the 7,000 letters in the first range of text or from the 7,000 letters in the last range of text. Now suppose that the frequency of alefs, khets and dalets within those 14,000 letters of the literal text were dramatically less than in the ranges of the 6,000 letters from which the Eckad ELSs with skips of 9,000 to 9,999 had to be drawn. Then this would cause, all by itself, a seemingly dramatic mosaic effect within that skip size range.

At first glance, the above concern seemed to discredit the purported significance of mosaics of any kind. For some skeptics, their work had been done, and the whole thing could be dismissed. Looking further, however, there were various considerations that argued against dismissal:

- First, the above concern is quite small for small skip size ranges. It does, however, grow for each category of successively longer skips.

- Second, BCD presented the results of a study of the relationship between the relative meaningfulness of different ELSs and how strong the mosaic effect was within Genesis 1-17 (February and March 2002 issues). The more often a given Hebrew word appeared in the literal text of the Bible, the more "meaningful" it was judged to be. And the greater the percentage variations of the actual number of occurrences were from the expected number, the more pronounced was the mosaic effect. This strong relationship restored some credibility to the concept after criticisms posed by skeptics. Nevertheless, the whole phenomenon was a bit complicated in the first place, and it didn't help to have to offer complex explanations for why it was still worth noting, even though its existence could be shown, in many instances, to be significantly due to seemingly chance variations in letter frequencies between different parts of the search text.

- Third, in the January 2001 issue, BCD put forth the concept of the author of the Bible as an incomparable chess master who had deliberately built in the major differences in letter frequencies between subsections of a search text in order to create the presence of mosaics for some ELSs. This concept was bolstered by the strong correlation between ELS meaningfulness and the strength of its mosaic effect.

- In the September 2002 issue, we noted the presence of the significant David mosaic in 1 Samuel.

  In the October 2002 issue and the January 2003 issue, we reported on some of the research conducted by David Bauscher in the Aramaic New Testament (the Peshitta). In the September 2003 issue, we reported on yet more of Bauscher's research, reviewing results for 29 different divine names as ELSs.

  In the fall of 2003 and the winter of 2004, a number of Bible code researchers focused on quantifying the primary weakness of the mosaic phenomenon, and searched for solutions to addressing this weakness. The basic problem, as detailed above, was this: the higher the skip size, the greater the proportion of the search text that would never be accessed by any of the ELSs within a given skip size range. And yet, when code software computes the expected number of occurrences, it uses the letter frequencies for the entire range of the search text.

  Bauscher set forth a potential solution for this—mosaic searches should be done using a wrapped text. In such a text, when you come to the end of the literal text, you start all over with another copy of that text. This approach is analogous to treating the search text as a cylinder rather than a long straight line. Using a wrapped text fully eliminates the valid concern of skeptics. For each skip size range, all ranges of the letters of the original search text were equal candidates for being part of the selected ELS. So, there is no longer any bias in the estimation of the expected number of occurrences of the given ELS with skips in a specified skip range.

The Controversy Over Mosaics: Round Five
Continued

Let There Be Light

In this issue, we present one of the most striking of Bauscher's intriguing findings based on wrapped text searches—again using a divine name for the ELSs to be examined. Bauscher has posted the results of a broad range of his research on his web site: http://aramaicnt.com

We will look at Bauscher's search results for the Hebrew word for light, OWR (Alef-Vav-Resh). The following graph provides a comparison of the Z-Values of the deviations of the actual number of occurrences from the expected number, for a full range of skip size categories. The Z-Value is the actual difference divided by the square root of the expected number of occurrences. If the Light mosaic from the Peshitta behaved in the same manner as the Light mosaic from the control text, virtually all of the Z-Values would fall within the range of -3 through +3. And the Z-Values would randomly vary above and below zero. In great contrast to this, 27 of the 46 Z-Values (or 58.7%) from the Peshitta text fall outside the range of values from the control text.

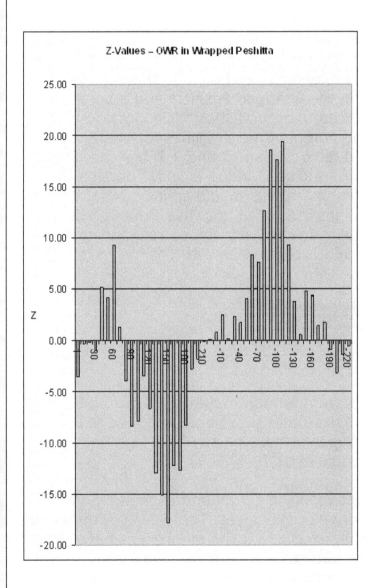

And the Z-Values form a wave pattern much like that of a light wave—which is most curious since this is the mosaic of the Hebrew word for light.

The next graph shows the results from the control text as a comparison. Its scale is the same as that for the Light mosaic graph from the Peshitta. Obviously, the control Z-Values are truly miniscule by comparison and are randomly positive or negative.

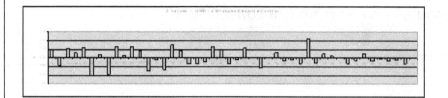

The above mosaics summarize comparisons of the differences between the expected and actual number of occurrences of the Light ELS in the wrapped Peshitta and a parallel control text. Within each, the Light ELS is expected to occur 130.3 million times—with skips of 1,000 or greater. Given the law of large numbers the Z-Values for nearly all the differences between actual and expected should fall between -3 and +3. Instead, the Z-Value for Light ELSs with positive skips is -20.58. Such a Z-Value is so far outside the range of results anticipated for random phenomena that we should conclude that it cannot be due to chance. And the Z-Value for Light ELSs with negative skips is +24.21, even further outside the range of expected results. In contrast, the corresponding Z-Values for the control text are quite small (+0.36 for Light ELSs with positive skips, and -0.21 for negative skips.

Sign of Skip	Expected	Peshitta Actual	Difference	Z-Value	Control Actual	Difference	Z-Value
Positive	65,154,353	64,988,227	-166,126	-20.58	65,157,299	2,946	0.36
Negative	65,154,353	65,349,809	195,456	24.21	65,152,669	-1,684	-0.21
ALL	130,308,706	130,338,036	29,330	2.57	130,309,968	1,262	0.11

In considering the size of the radical departures from random behavior exhibited by the Light mosaic in the Peshitta, it should be emphasized that by using a wrapped text, any bias due to differences in letter frequencies between various parts of the text has been eliminated. And yet, this powerfully striking mosaic exists!

The next table shows the specific differences between the actual and expected number of occurrences of the Light ELS for the entire range of skip sizes. The values in this table directly correspond to those in the above graphs, except that the differences have been converted to Z-values. For each of the skip size ranges, the expected number of occurrences of the Light ELS is 2,845,167. An exception is the first skip size range, which is smaller, ranging only from 1,000 to 10,000—while all of the positive skip size ranges are 10,000 wide. Another exception is the first negative skip size range (i.e., that for -1,000 to -10,000). For each of these, the expected number of occurrences of the Light ELS is 2,560,679.

Divine Contact-The Original New Testament Discovered

Minimum Skip (000's)	Maximum Skip (000's)	Actual Difference	Control Difference	Minimum Skip (000's)	Maximum Skip (000's)	Actual Difference	Control Difference
1	10	-5,576	1,480	-1	-10	1,266	-276
10	20	-470	-1,495	-10	-20	4,248	1,918
20	30	-338	1,755	-20	-30	294	-92
30	40	-1,642	879	-30	-40	3,915	-1,886
40	50	8,682	1,920	-40	-50	2,984	-132
50	60	7,133	-3,470	-50	-60	6,912	902
60	70	15,679	614	-60	-70	14,045	-655
70	80	2,268	-3,275	-70	-80	12,851	-402
80	90	-6,582	2,162	-80	-90	21,380	-1,032
90	100	-14,092	319	-90	-100	31,429	3,606
100	110	-13,286	2,195	-100	-110	29,751	-885
110	120	-5,790	1,324	-110	-120	32,681	726
120	130	-11,152	-2,533	-120	-130	15,657	359
130	140	-21,829	-302	-130	-140	6,405	1
140	150	-25,445	-2,222	-140	-150	962	-1,072
150	160	-30,101	2,561	-150	-160	8,029	-530
160	170	-20,637	1,391	-160	-170	7,343	784
170	180	-21,416	-1,173	-170	-180	2,488	-656
180	190	-13,911	-1,130	-180	-190	2,912	-261
190	200	-4,644	-726	-190	-200	-1,510	-655
200	210	-3,093	2,242	-200	-210	-5,421	-402
210	220	-84	1,685	-210	-220	-2,211	-1,032
220	230	200	-1,255	-220	-230	-954	-12

Conducting mosaic searches in wrapped texts appears to hold great promise in providing compelling evidence of the inspired origin of the Aramaic New Testament. It will also be interesting to apply this approach to the Hebrew Old Testament, as well as to the Torah alone.

Here is another article on my research, published in October , 2003 on the same topic :

Striking Evidence of Intentional Encoding in the Aramaic New Testament

Extensive new findings by researcher Rev. Glenn David Bauscher of Cambridge, New York provide some of the most striking and statistically significant evidence of encoding yet discovered. The search text is the Aramaic New Testament (Peshitta) and the evidence consists of a series of dramatic mosaics, which are comprised of highly improbable variations from expected in the number of times a given ELS appears in a text. In this article we will focus entirely on 29 different four-letter-long divine names. Bauscher has also conducted extensive research on mosaics for three-, five- and six-letter-long divine names as well, but space doesn't allow for presentation of the full range of his research in this issue.

In the October 2002 issue we first reported on some quite striking mosaics discovered by researcher Bauscher in the Peshitta. Those mosaics were comprised of highly improbable variations in the number of appearances of three four-letter names of God.

Divine Contact-The Original New Testament Discovered

In the <u>January, 2003 issue</u> we presented another compelling Bauscher mosaic comprised of occurrences of Yeshu (Jesus) as an ELS in the Peshitta.

For each of the 29 four-letter-long divine names, Bauscher also conducted exactly parallel searches in a scrambled text of the Peshitta provided by researcher Roy Reinhold for Codefinder. The total number of forward and backward occurrences of each of the ELSs were recorded for all skips from 1,000 up to the maximum possible skip size (153,633). In each case a comparison was made between the expected total number of occurrences and the actual number. This provided a set of 58 variations from expected from both the Peshitta and the scrambled (control) text.

For example, the Aramaic equivalent of the Hebrew word for God, Elohim, is Alaha. Alaha appears as an ELS 2,718,407 times in the Peshitta with a positive skip between 1,000 and 153,633. The Alaha ELS appears 135,567 times more often than expected by chance. This is an exceptionally large variation—given how large the expected number of occurrences is, and the inexorable nature of the Law of Large Numbers. That law will cause variations from the expected to be a smaller percentage of the expected as the expected number itself becomes larger. In the case of the Alaha example, the average variation from expected due to chance is 20,386, so the actual variation is 6.65 times greater than that. What this means is that the variation from expected should almost always be less than three times the average variation from expected, or 61,158 (3 x 20,386), and yet it is 135,567, which is dramatically greater.

In the following chart, the ELSs with the most improbable variations from expected are presented in descending order. The relative size of a variation from expected is measured in terms of a "Z Value." It is the ratio of the actual variation from expected to the average variation from expected that normally occurs.

Divine Contact-The Original New Testament Discovered

Rank	Text	English Transliteration -- Aramaic Translation	Skips	Absolute Value of Z Score
1	Peshitta	Alaha "God" (Elohim)	Pos	84.35
2	Peshitta	Mariah "Yahweh"	Neg	74.19
3	Peshitta	Cohena "The Priest"	Pos	73.40
4	Peshitta	YAHEL= "LORD God"	Pos	73.08
5	Peshitta	Ruacha "The Spirit"	Pos	61.29
6	Peshitta	Ruacha "The Spirit"	Neg	60.84
7	Peshitta	ELYAH "God The LORD"	Neg	56.67
8	Peshitta	ELYAH "God The LORD"	Pos	55.64
9	Peshitta	Yahweh	Neg	51.34
10	Peshitta	Meltha "The Word"	Neg	48.53
11	Peshitta	Chiim "Life, Salvation"	Pos	48.08
12	Peshitta	Ha Ruach "The Spirit"	Neg	47.89
13	Peshitta	Ha Emeth "The Truth"	Pos	47.88
14	Peshitta	Adonai "The Lord"	Neg	43.65
15	Peshitta	Ha Emeth "The Truth"	Neg	41.30
16	Peshitta	Yahweh	Pos	40.68
17	Peshitta	Chiim "Life, Salvation"	Neg	39.73
18	Peshitta	Alaha "God" (Elohim)	Neg	37.03
19	Peshitta	Shemia "Heaven", or "God"	Neg	34.85
20	Peshitta	Sarera "The Truth"	Neg	32.19
21	Peshitta	Shemia "Heaven", or "God"	Pos	31.74
22	Peshitta	Meshiach "Messiah"	Neg	30.80
23	Peshitta	Ha Ruach "The Spirit"	Pos	29.72
24	Peshitta	Machin "Savior"	Pos	27.06
25	Peshitta	Meltha "The Word"	Pos	26.78
26	Peshitta	Ha Melek "The King"	Pos	23.76
27	Peshitta	Chuva "Love"	Pos	23.72
28	Peshitta	Meshiach "Messiah"	Pos	22.00
29	W&P	Amin "The Amen"	Pos	20.85
30	Peshitta	Amin "The Amen"	Pos	19.07
31	Peshitta	49 Ha Dabar "The Word"	Neg	18.47
32	Peshitta	YAHEL "LORD God"	Neg	18.35
33	W&P	Ha Amen "The Amen"	Pos	18.27
34	Peshitta	Chasik "Thine Holy One"	Pos	18.17
35	Peshitta	Mariah "Yahweh"	Pos	17.61
36	W&P	Alaha "God" (Elohim)	Pos	17.48
37	Peshitta	Ha Melah "The Word"	Pos	16.37
38	Peshitta	Machin "Savior"	Neg	14.99
39	Peshitta	Ha Melek "The King"	Neg	14.43

38	Peshitta	Machin "Savior"	Neg	14.99
39	Peshitta	Ha Melek "The King"	Neg	14.43
40	W&P	Adonai "The Lord"	Neg	14.41
41	Peshitta	Elama "The Eternal"	Pos	11.90
42	Peshitta	Chasik "Thine Holy One"	Neg	11.79
43	Peshitta	Ha Derek "The Way"	Pos	11.70
44	Peshitta	Yeshua "Jesus"	Pos	11.40
45	Peshitta	Ha Amen "The Amen"	Pos	11.37
46	Peshitta	Yeshua "Jesus"	Neg	9.68
47	Peshitta	Amin "The Amen"	Neg	9.34
48	W&P	Ha Emeth "The Truth"	Neg	8.64
49	W&P	Chiim "Life, Salvation"	Pos	8.33
50	Peshitta	Pharuq "Savior"	Pos	8.31
51	W&P	Meltha "The Word"	Pos	8.27
52	Peshitta	Shamim "Heaven"	Neg	7.86
53	W&P	Shamim "Heaven"	Pos	6.90
54	W&P	Ha Emeth "The Truth"	Pos	6.67
55	W&P	Cohena "The Priest"	Pos	6.53
56	W&P	Elama "The Eternal"	Neg	6.13
57	Peshitta	Ha Dabar "The Word"	Pos	5.71
58	W&P	Ha Amen "The Amen"	Neg	5.68
59	Peshitta	Shamim "Heaven"	Pos	5.66
60	Peshitta	Ha Derek - "The Way"	Neg	5.64
61	W&P	Yahweh	Pos	5.50
62	W&P	Yeshua "Jesus"	Neg	5.25
63	Peshitta	Chuva "Love"	Neg	5.24
64	Peshitta	Sarera "The Truth"	Pos	5.22
65	W&P	Adonai "The Lord"	Pos	5.21
66	Peshitta	Qadosh "Holy One"	Neg	5.13
67	W&P	Shemia "Heaven", or "God"	Pos	5.05
68	W&P	Ha Derek "The Way"	Neg	4.94
69	W&P	Shemia "Heaven", or "God"	Neg	4.72
70	W&P	Meshiach "Messiah"	Pos	4.57
71	W&P	Ha Melek "The King"	Pos	4.50
72	W&P	YAHEL "LORD God"	Pos	4.36
73	Peshitta	Qadosh "Holy One"	Pos	4.22
74	W&P	Ruacha "The Spirit"	Pos	4.05
75	W&P	Chuva "Love"	Pos	3.99
76	Peshitta	Pharuq "Savior"	Neg	3.91
77	W&P	Ha Melah "The Word"	Neg	3.68
78	W&P	Chasik "Thine Holy One"	Pos	3.48
79	W&P	Chasik "Thine Holy One"	Neg	3.37
80	W&P	Chiim "Life, Salvation"	Neg	3.11

81	W&P	Mariah "Yahweh"	Neg	3.07
82	W&P	Alaha "God" (Elohim)	Neg	2.80
83	W&P	Ha Melah "The Word"	Pos	2.78
84	W&P	Machin "Savior"	Neg	2.75
85	Peshitta	Elama "The Eternal"	Neg	2.60
86	W&P	Ha Dabar "The Word"	Pos	2.32
87	W&P	Meltha "The Word"	Neg	2.27
88	W&P	Ruacha "The Spirit"	Neg	2.16
89	W&P	Meshiach "Messiah"	Neg	2.16
90	Peshitta	Adonai "The Lord"	Pos	2.00
91	W&P	ELYAH "God The LORD"	Neg	1.98
92	W&P	Sarera "The Truth"	Pos	1.88
93	W&P	Pharuq "Savior"	Neg	1.81
94	Peshitta	Ha Amen "The Amen"	Neg	1.57
95	W&P	Mariah "Yahweh"	Pos	1.46
96	W&P	Qadosh "Holy One"	Pos	1.44
97	Peshitta	Ha Melah "The Word"	Neg	1.29
98	W&P	Machin "Savior"	Pos	1.13
99	W&P	Yeshua "Jesus"	Pos	0.86
100	W&P	YAHEL "LORD God"	Neg	0.83
101	W&P	Qadosh "Holy One"	Neg	0.82
102	W&P	Chuva "Love"	Neg	0.81
103	W&P	Ha Dabar "The WORD"	Neg	0.68
104	W&P	Elama "The Eternal"	Pos	0.63
105	W&P	Shamim "Heaven"	Neg	0.63
106	W&P	Cohena "The Priest"	Neg	0.62
107	W&P	ELYAH "God The LORD"	Pos	0.61
108	W&P	Pharuq "Savior"	Pos	0.51
109	W&P	Ha Derek "The Way"	Pos	0.37
110	W&P	Sarera "The Truth"	Neg	0.18
111	W&P	Amin "The Amen"	Neg	0.14
112	W&P	Ha Ruach "The Spirit"	Pos	0.11
113	W&P	Yahweh	Neg	0.11
114	W&P	Ha Melek "The King"	Neg	0.09
115	Peshitta	Cohena "The Priest"	Neg	0.05
116	W&P	Ha Ruach "The Spirit"	Neg	0.05

In visually reviewing the above chart, it is immediately obvious that the top of the chart is completely dominated by Peshitta findings. <u>All of the top 28 ELSs with the most improbable Z scores are from the Peshitta text</u>. Furthermore, 44 out of the 50 ELSs with the most improbable Z scores are from the Peshitta text. Conversely, the bottom is heavily populated with findings from the control text. The next table summarizes this.

Comparison of the Number of Findings in Each Category of Rankings (Rankings Based on Relative Improbability of Random Occurrence)		
Rankings	Peshitta	Control
1-20	20	0
21-40	16	4
41-60	12	8
61-80	5	15
81-100	4	16
101-116	1	19

Of the twenty mosaics that are the most improbable, all are from the Peshitta. Of the mosaics that ranked between 21st and 40th in improbability, 16 are from the Peshitta and 4 from the control text.

In the next table we separately sorted all of the Z scores from the Peshitta and from the control text and we took the ratio of the Z scores of the equally ranked Z scores.

Ranked Z Scores from:		Ratio of Equally
Peshitta	**Control**	**Ranked Z Scores**
0.99624188	0.9858979	0.733637556
84.4	20.9	4
74.2	18.3	4.1
73.4	17.5	4.2
73.1	14.4	5.1
61.3	8.6	7.1
60.8	8.3	7.3
56.7	8.3	6.9
55.6	6.9	8.1

51.3	6.7	7.7
48.5	6.5	7.4
48.1	6.1	7.8
47.9	5.7	8.4
47.9	5.5	8.7
43.7	5.3	8.3
41.3	5.2	7.9
40.7	5.1	8
39.7	4.9	8
37	4.7	7.8
34.9	4.6	7.6
32.2	4.5	7.2
31.7	4.4	7.3
30.8	4.1	7.6
29.7	4	7.4
27.1	3.7	7.4
26.8	3.5	7.7
23.8	3.4	7.1
23.7	3.1	7.6
22	3.1	7.2
19.1	2.8	6.8
18.5	2.8	6.6
18.3	2.8	6.7
18.2	2.3	7.8
17.6	2.3	7.8
16.4	2.2	7.6
15	2.2	6.9
14.4	2	7.3
11.9	1.9	6.3
11.8	1.8	6.5
11.7	1.5	8
11.4	1.4	7.9
11.4	1.1	10.1
9.7	0.9	11.2
9.3	0.8	11.2
8.3	0.8	10.2
7.9	0.8	9.7
5.7	0.7	8.4
5.7	0.6	9
5.6	0.6	9
5.2	0.6	8.5
5.2	0.6	8.5
5.1	0.5	10
4.2	0.4	11.5

3.9	0.2	22.1
2.6	0.1	19
2	0.1	17.5
1.6	0.1	14.6
1.3	0.1	14
0.1	0	1.2

Several observations can be made about the above table.

- First, the degree of variation exhibited by the Z scores of the four-letter divine names in the control text is much larger than would be expected if those Z scores conformed to a normal distribution (i.e., a bell-shaped curve). This is largely due to the fact that there is often a sizeable correlation between the size and sign of variations from expected for any given ELS over adjacent skip ranges. This is caused by local variations in letter frequencies for different areas of the literal text.

- Second, having 58 Z scores (variations from expected) from a control text provides a clear definition of the degree of variation in Z scores expected by chance.

- Third, typically the Peshitta Z score is 6 to 10 times greater than the corresponding control text Z score—when these Z scores are ranked from the greatest to the smallest.

- This is very compelling evidence of the existence of intentional encoding, no matter how one goes about estimating the probability of chance occurrence.

Bauscher's research has provided a dramatic, clear-cut example of a sacred text that conclusively exhibits the deliberate encoding of excess occurrences of several divine names. Clearly further research in this area is indicated, and Bauscher has already been exploring that with many additional interesting findings.

Technical Addendum:
The Conclusive Significance
of the Divine Name Mosaics in the Peshitta

Estimating the odds of chance occurrence of Bauscher's findings is complicated by certain key issues. As noted in the first bulleted point regarding the comparison of ranked Z scores, the distribution of Z values from the control text is more dispersed than would be indicated if mosaics conformed to a typical bell-shaped normal curve, or any one of several other common probability distributions. As mentioned above, this is due to the presence of correlation in many of the mosaics.

Bauscher's way of dealing with this has been to measure the degree of correlation in each mosaic and to exclude from the above comparison examples where the correlation is too high. This is helpful to a fair degree, but the problem is that the remaining examples from the control text are still too spread out to conform to a bell-shaped curve. This means that probabilities estimated by standard statistical tests that assume the presence of normally behaved phenomena will be inaccurate.

A solution to this problem is to apply a statistical test that makes no assumptions about the statistical nature of the underlying phenomenon. Such a test is termed a non-parametric test. The Wilcoxen-Mann-Whitney test is one of the most widely accepted tests of this type. As intimidating as the name of this test is, it is actually simple to understand. First we rank the Z scores of all of Bauscher's findings for four-letter-long divine names—exactly as they appear in the left column of the first table above. Then we sum up the ranks of the Peshitta findings. That total is 2,091, and we will call it the "ranksum." If the Peshitta results were totally unremarkable, the rankings of the Peshitta results and the control results would be randomly dispersed among one another. The sum of all of the rankings is 6,786, so the expected value of the rank sum of all the Peshitta findings should be exactly half of that, or 3,393. This makes sense because, for example, if all of the Peshitta findings had rankings that were odd numbers (i.e., 1,3,5,7,.....111,113,115) the ranksum would be 3,364. And if all of the Peshitta findings had rankings that were even numbers, the ranksum would be 3,422.

It so happens that the ranksum statistic becomes normally distributed as the sample size becomes large. So the ranksum conforms to a bell shaped curve, and the average variation from expected (commonly called the standard deviation) is the square root of $(1/12)mn(m+n+1)$, where m and n are the number of observations from the Peshitta and the control text [see page 437 of Statistical Theory, by B.W. Lindgren, 2nd Edition, Macmillan, 1968]. Thus the standard deviation is 181.1049, and the Z-value of the Peshitta ranksum is 7.189 (=(3,393-2,091)/181.1049). Given a normal bell-shaped curve, this means that the odds of chance occurrence of the Peshitta findings are less than 1 in 3.047 trillion. So we can conclusively reject the hypothesis that the Peshitta findings are due to chance.

The Peshitta findings are far more improbable than the Wilcoxen test indicates, however. In statistical language, a non-parametric test is not very efficient. In other words, it only tells us that the odds are clearly "less than" some value, but it doesn't provide us with an accurate estimate of the exact odds. This doesn't really matter, however, because the odds indicated by the test are already so remote that we should conclusively reject chance as an explanation of the results.

One thing that the Wilcoxen test doesn't measure adequately is that the Peshitta Z scores are not only higher in general than the control Z scores, they are typically far greater. To appreciate this, suppose we took all of the Peshitta Z scores and we cut them in half. The resulting Peshitta ranksum would be 2,403, still far less than the control ranksum of 4,383, and the odds of chance occurrence of the halved Peshitta Z scores would still be less than 1 in 43,454,423. We would still very conclusively eliminate chance as an explanation. In fact, we could even reduce all the Peshitta Z scores by two-thirds and the odds of chance occurrence would still be less than 1 in 27,823.

Below is a sample from the Divine Names experiment. This is the last Name searched in the Peshitta:

ברא "Bara" (Aramaic- "The Son")								
skips/-1000's	expected	actual	deviation	sq rt expect.	Stand. dev.	Log of Prob.	Chi ^{2}	
1-30	3460158	3453018	7140	1860.149994	3.838	-4.098	14.733	
30-60	3579470	3576078	3392	1891.948731	1.793	-1.597	3.214	
60-90	3579470	3581167	1697	1891.948731	0.897	-1.074	0.805	
90-120	3579470	3597124	17654	1891.948731	9.331	-19.804	87.070	
120-150	3579470	3612919	33449	1891.948731	17.680	-68.766	312.570	
150-180	3579470	3613097	33627	1891.948731	17.774	-69.490	315.906	
180-210	3579470	3611244	31774	1891.948731	16.794	-62.139	282.049	
210-230	2386353	2401244	14891	1544.782509	9.640	-21.074	92.921	
		Totals for 367 searches: Avg. P = -6.01	42%Z's> 3					
						Chi ^{2}	8627.9	
						Avg. Z	4.85	
						count	367	

ברא "Bara" (Aramaic- "The Son") in the scrambled Peshitta control text

expected	actual	avg. dev.	Sq Rt exp	St. Dev.	Log of P	Chi ^{2}			
3460158	3457870	2288	1860.15	1.230008337	-1.22758239	1.512920508			
3579470	3579676	206	1891.9487	0.108882443	-0.90166403	0.011855386			
3579470	3577471	1999	1891.9487	1.056582542	-1.14148074	1.116366669			
3579470	3576069	3401	1891.9487	1.797617422	-1.60071294	3.231428396			
3579470	3581108	1638	1891.9487	0.865773989	-1.06183894	0.7495646			
3579470	3578974	496	1891.9487	0.262163552	-0.91401286	0.068729728			
3579470	3583144	3674	1891.9487	1.941913087	-1.71787302	3.771026437			
2386353	2388144	1791	1544.7825	1.159386509	-1.19094401	1.344177077			
		Totals for 367 searches:		Avg. P= -1.04; 0.27% Z's > 3					
					Chi ^{2}	351.244			
					Avg. Z	0.98			

The far left column shows the skip rate for the search term (in thousands of letters skipped) which I searched with CodeFinder 1.22.

CodeFinder will search any text which has been formatted for the program for any term with two or more letters, by skipping letters in that text.

The skip number may be set in the program for different range limits - 1 to 100,000 , for example.

Divine Contact-The Original New Testament Discovered

The second column from the left shows what the "expected" number of ELS's is to be found in a particular search.

The third column shows the "actual" result of the search for a particular term at a certain skip range.

The fourth column shows "deviation", which is simply the difference between Expected and Actual results (with only positive values , absolute, of that difference).

The fifth column shows the square root of the expected value. This is used in calculating a probability for the actual number of ELS's (ELS's are the words that show up as a result of a search.

The sixth column is the Standard Deviation, which is a statistic used to represent a probability for an event. It is the deviation divided by the square root of the expected number of ELS's. Another term for the Standard Deviation is the Z Score. A Z score will normally be a number less than 2.0, almost always (95% of the time) less than 3.0.

The seventh column is the Logarithm of Probabilty. There is a formula to determine the probability represented by a Z Score , into which I will not go here. The Log of P for 50% probability would be -0.30. A 10% Probability would be -1.0 . A 1% Prob. Has a Log of -2.0. A 0.1% (1 in 1000) has a Log of -3.0, etc.

A Z Score of 1 represents about a 1 in 10 probability; 2 is approx 1 in 100; 3 is approx. 1 in 1000. Beyond 3.0, the probabilities start to decrease exponentially. A Z Score of 4 shows a Probability of 1 in 33,000. A Z Score of 5 represents 1 in 3.5 million !

A Z Score of 6 is 1 in a billion !

The Chi Squared total is the standard method by which to calculate probability. That total for the Control text is 351 for 367 searches. A Chi Square is simply a Z score squared.

The Chi Squared total for a normal array of non coded material should be close to the number of searches, which is 367.

A Chi Squared of 351 is completely normal and indicates a non coded text for the scrambled Peshitta Control text.

Every one of the 367 Peshitta searches is matched with a Control search in a scrambled Peshitta NT text of exactly the same size.It has the same letter frequencies and the search ranges are identical in both texts, with the same words searched in both texts.The Z Score is the number of Standard Deviations of actual occurrences of ELS's (# occurrences of search words) from the Expected number of ELS's.

For example, the last search done above is the Aramaic word **"Bra" (Son)** at skips 210,000 to 230,000. That search found 2,401,244 occurrences of "Bra" by skipping 210,000 letters & up to 230,000 letters between each of the three Aramaic letters of **"B" "R" "A"**. The Expected number of occurrences in a normal non-coded text is 2,386,353. The difference between the actual & expected is 14,891.

One standard deviation is calculated as the square root of the expected number; the Sq. Rt. of 2,386,353 is 1544.78.

Notice at the far right in the lavendar shaded data that the control search found 2,388,144 of the same ELS of "Bra" in the scrambled Peshitta text. That is 1.16 Standard Deviations. 0 to 2 Standard Deviations is considered normal. The Peshitta search yielded 9.64 Standard Deviations; The Z Score is then 9.64.

A 9.64 Z Score represents a probability of one in 10^{20}, or 1 in 100,000,000,000,000,000,000.

The Average Z Score of **4.85** per ELS represents a probability of 1 in 1.64 million ! The composite probability for all the searches would be 10^{-2204}. That is one in 10^{2204}, which is an outrageously small probability. One may as well say the probabilty is zero that these Name ELS's are unintentional.

Codecracker generally confirms the results of my Divine Names experiment.

Testing the ten largest NT books eliminates the effect of repetition of common phrases used in the four Gospels and in the epistles, which repetition can mimic a code effect, as Randy showed exists in the book of Numbers (See his book, Who Wrote The Bible Code).I also disregarded ELS's below skip numbers of 100 in averaging Z Scores. For Digram Chi squared Scores, I used only Z Scores for skips above 500.

The averages for the whole NT, using skips 2-100,000 , for trigram entropy and digrams chi squared, are **2.82** (high,but below the significant **3.0**) for The Byzantine Greek NT , and **4.22** for The Peshitta NT. The rather high score for the Greek NT is probably due to the repetition noted above. It would also raise The Peshitta score somewhat.The tests of ten individual books pretty much eliminates the effect of repetition of phrases which occurs in similar books (Four similar Gospels and 21 similar epistles).

I welcome those who are interested to examine the texts of both the OLD AND NEW TESTAMENTS for long and short codes of the type I have mentioned. I call the latter –mini codes. They seem to be *the Divine watermark of the scriptures in the Hebrew and Aramaic texts.*
The results from two large arrays totaling over 1200 data points yield a Cumulative **Z Score of 100**; a total probability of less than 10^{-2100}.

The total results for findings in <u>The Peshitta Names of God Experiment</u> have a probability equivalent to flipping a coin 20,000 times and getting heads every time !
This is just a small sample of the coded information in the entire New Testament! (See probability for Matthew above).

Chapter 13
<u>Guess Who Wrote The Bible Code ?</u>

These following data and resulting statistics represent a test of my Divine Names experiment in **The Peshitta NT** using Randy Ingermanson's CodeCracker software, described in his book, **Who Wrote The Bible Code?**
He concluded that no codes (or very few) exist in The Hebrew OT.
His experiment tested only individual books.
I have found highly significant results, testing The Torah as a unit and also The Peshitta Aramaic New Testament as a unit, hitherto never done, to my knowledge.

CodeCracker, Randy Ingermanson's software gives a 4.67 Z Score for The Peshitta NT for skips 200-1000 for all Trigrams (3 letter Hebrew-Aramaic word patterns).

Here is an excerpt from his program's output for The Peshitta's book of Acts:

 # Beginning analysis of file: Acts Peshitto Codefinder.txt
 # Today's date: Fri Jul 16 11:46:06 EDT 2004
#
 # Maximum number of lines to read: 50000
 # File data is: Hebrew text
#
 # Total number of lines   read: 2

\# Total number of characters   read: 65814
\# Total number of words   read: 1
\# Total number of distinct words read: 1
\#
\# Smallest word size: 65813
\# Largest word size: 65813
\#
\# Analysis type: Entropy analysis of trigrams
\#
\# The alphabet being used has 22 distinct characters.
\# Total number of letters read: 65813
\# Number of distinct letters read: 22
\#
\# Maximal Letter Entropy of the text: 4.459431618637297
\# Actual Letter Entropy of the text: 4.0102141742353306
\#
\# Total number of trigrams read: 65811
\# Number of distinct trigrams read: 5011
\#
\# Theoretical Trigram Entropy of the text: 3.9714353285043433
\# Actual   Trigram Entropy of the text: 3.631719202460799
\#
\#
\# The seed used for the random number generator was: 0
\# The text was randomized in bins of size: 250
\#
\# Lowest skip studied is 1
\# Highest skip studied is 20000
\# Difference between successive skips is 1
\# Difference between successive thresholds is 10
\#
Here is the average entropy for all original skip-texts:
3.971982611245521 +/- 1.8292689913043477E-5
(Standard deviation = 0.0025869770167311597).

Here is the average entropy for all randomized texts:
3.9720339390818205 +/- 3.6307884002217256E-6
(Standard deviation = 5.134710197700477E-4).

Now let's see if the skip-texts are essentially random beyond
some threshold skip. A typical threshold skip is 50 to 100.
We'll consider the result highly significant if we find a
Z-score greater than 5.0, unless there is some good
explanation for the high Z-score.

See my book "Who Wrote the Bible Code?" for details.

If we take a threshold of 100, the skip-texts beyond it have
an average entropy of: 3.9720089972781847 +/- 3.6306546790114183E-6
Relative to the randomized texts, these skip-texts have a
Z-score of -4.8513991394761256

I show this result because the threshold of 100 skipped letters is normally the minimum recommended for
computing Z Scores by Randy and which I normally observed for my experiments with Codecracker.
4.85 is exactly the value I obtained for my Divine Names experiment as I pointed out above.

Matthew has a **3.85** according to Codecracker.	3.85	1.59	6.1215
Mark has **3.63** according to Codecracker.	3.63	1	3.63
Luke has **5.14** according to Codecracker.	5.14	1.72	8.8408
John has **3.28** according to Codecracker.	3.28	1.37	4.4936
Acts has **4.85** according to Codecracker.	4.85	1.81	8.7785
	4.15	1.498	31.8644

A weighted avg. for book size for these five books gives a **4.7916** **Z Score**

4.792 is just **0.01 less than the average from the original experiment !**
So Randy Ingermanson's program seems to verify my original results as reliable.

Ten New Testament books tested for coding in The Peshitta and Byzantine Greek Majority text, using Codecracker 1.0, developed by Randy Ingermanson:

3.43 is the Average Z Score for the Codefinder version of ten individual Peshitta NT books,
as calculated by Ingermanson's Codecracker software. Each book was analyzed at
at nearly all possible skip ranges. Mark, for example, was searched at skips 1 to 12,000,
for trigrams (3 letter word patterns).

The following NT books were searched with Codecracker at all possible skip numbers in The Peshitta
and in The Majority Greek Text (also called The Byzantine Text).

	Peshitta NT	Peshitta NT Digram & Trigram Entropy	Peshitta NT Digram & Trigram Entropy	Peshitta NT Digram - TrigramZ Score	Peshitta NT Digram – Trigram X^2	Greek NT Digram – Trigram	Greek NT Digram - Trigrams	Greek NT Digrams
Book	Z Scores > 3.0	Avg.Ent. Z Score	Entropy X^2	Digram Z	Digram X^2	Avg. Greek Z	Digram X^2	X^2 TestZ
Mat	13.60%	3.82	14.59	3.4	*11.56*	4.94	24.4	1.11 *1.23*
Mark	51%	3.63	13.18	3	*9*	0.87	0.76	0.85 *0.72*
Luke	99%	5.14	26.42	5	*25*	0.31	0.1	0.58 *0.34*
John	9%	3.49	12.18	3.71	*13.7641*	1.2	1.44	1.34 *1.8*
Acts	58%	4.85	23.52	3.85	*14.8225*	1.4	1.96	1.08 *1.17*
Romans	54%	3.88	15.05	2.36	*5.5696*	2.81	7.9	3.1 *9.61*
1 Cor	6.40%	3.67	13.47	2.86	*8.1796*	2.62	6.86	1.48 *2.19*
2 Cor	0%	2.77	7.67	1	*1*	2.77	7.67	0.67 *0.45*
Hebrews	0%	3.38	11.42	3	*9*	3.86	14.9	2.25 *5.06*
Rev	72.86%	4.52	20.43	2.4	*5.76*	0.78	0.61	3.2 *10.2*
Avg Z's >3	**36.39%**	**3.92**	**3.97**	**3.06**	*3.22*	**2.16**	**2.58 1.57**	*1.81*

Divine Contact-The Original New Testament Discovered

	Pesh.NT	Z Score	# skip texts(Trigrams)		Byz. Greek	Z Score	# skip texts(Trigrams)	
	Mat	3.60	19000		Mat	2.34	33000	
	Mark	3.30	7000		Mark	0.86	19000	
	Luke	5.07	20000		Luke	0.42	27000	
	John	3.60	15000		John	1.27	16000	
	Acts	4.32	20000		Acts	1.23	20000	
	Romans	3.03	7000		Romans	2.95	7000	
	1 Cor	3.24	7000		1 Cor	1.97	11000	
	2 Cor	1.66	5000		2 Cor	1.36	5000	
	Hebrews	3.18	7000		Hebrews	2.95	7000	
	Rev	3.29	7000		Rev	1.58	15000	
		3.43	114000			1.69	160000	

Codecracker should yield the same results with entropy tests as with chi squared tests. As it is, I have averaged the results of both, multiplying Z scores of each and taking the Sq. Rt. of the product.
3.43 is the Average Z Score for the Codefinder version of ten individual Peshitta NT books, as calculated by Ingermanson's Codecracker software. Each book was analyzed at nearly all possible skip ranges. Mark, for example, was searched at skips 1 to 12,000 for trigrams (3 letter word patterns).
Trigrams were searched at up to 1/3 the total number of letters for max. skip rate. Codecracker gives unreliable results for searches beyond that level. Digrams were searched at up to 1/2 the total # letters in the text.
Each book was searched at least twice, once for digram chi squared values and once for trigram entropy , or trigram chi squared values. Many books were searched three times or more. I have averaged the Z Scores for trigrams (3 letter patterns) and digrams (2 letter patterns).

Randy Ingermanson , the author of Who Wrote The Bible Code ?, claimed that there is no code in the Bible, based on his searches of the Bible books using his Codecracker software. He has made his software publicly available and invites anyone to use it to search the Bible for codes. I have been doing so for several years now, and have found evidence that codes do exist in the Old Testament and in the New Testament. There is a major difference in our methods of searching the Bible; Randy's searches are limited to skip numbers 1 to 150. Most Bible books can be searched at skip numbers far higher than that. Even a small book like Jude in The NT , which is two pages long in English, can be searched at skips from 1 to 1200 in the Greek text. Most books are far larger than that , and can be searched at skips of about 8000. Randy's searches of the Old Testament cover only 1% of the search text ! How can that be a scientific experiment ? 1% of the possible data cannot prove anything. Randy seems to assume that if God were to put codes into the Bible, He would put codes in the text at all possible skip numbers, and if they do not show up at the bottom 1% of skip texts, then they must not exist in the other 99% of the texts ! How can we take him seriously ?

The Torah as a whole shows a code effect when searched at several thousand skip texts, averaging a one in several thousand probability per ELS (individual word found by skipping letters).

I have searched the New Testament in Greek and compared that to a search of The Aramaic NT, both as a whole and in ten individual books.
Each book is at least 12,000 letters long. I set the search maximum to half the text length for digrams (two letter combinations) and one third the text length for trigrams (three letter combinations).

Prior to using Randy's software, I performed an experiment , using The Peshitta New Testament , which was written in Aramaic , the language Jesus spoke. I searched the text for Divine names , found in the Hebrew

Divine Contact-The Original New Testament Discovered

Bible and in The Peshitta, in Hebrew and Aramaic. Aramaic and Hebrew share the same alphabet, therefore it is feasible to search for words in both languages in the same Aramaic text.

I searched for 95 Divine names and titles, to test the hypothesis that, **"If God were to put codes in The Bible, He would code it with His Names and Titles, as found in the books of The Old and New Testaments, as a Divine signature and watermark, signifying His authorship of the books and codes."**

The software I used was Codefinder, produced by Kevin Acres of Research Systems. It is probably the most powerful codebreaking software commercially available.I performed several trials of several thousand searches, comparing each Peshitta search with a control search.

The final trial consisted of 367 searches in The Peshitta and 367 in a control text (a scrambled Peshitta text of the same letter composition and size as The Peshitta).All possible search numbers were used, searching the NT as a whole.

The results were that the average ELS has a probability of 1 in 1.64 million !

The Actual number of occurrences of a word found in a search was compared to the expected number, based on a formula which calculated the expected number using the letter frequency tables for each word searched in that search text. It is a very accurate method, predicting results very reliably for control texts.

The control text had an average result per ELS of 1 in 14, or 7% . This is an entirely normal and expected result; it means there is no code in the control, or dummy text.

Interestingly, the straight or *"naïve"* average Z Score for the Names experiment is 3.35. The average using Codecracker ,shown above, is 3.43. A Z Score of 3.35 represents odds of 4.6 out of 10,000. 3.43 represents 3.5 in 10,000.

3.35 is a probability of **0.000462.**

3.43 is a probability of **0.000352.**

The Peshitta NT (Codefinder edition) , when searched for Digrams and analyzed by chi squared results, at skips 2-230,000, at every 11th skip (the time required for all skips is beyond my patience and my computer's data handling power), yields a Z Score average of 3.26 for skips beyond 1100 all the way out to skips beyond 8500. A Z Score of 3.26 represents odds of 6 out of 10,000.

The Digram Chi Squared search seems to be the most reliable of Codecracker's four methods of searching a text.

The comprehensive Digram Chi Squared NT search Z score avg. of 3.26 is very close to the 3.43 avg. for the 10 individual Peshitta books.

These results are very different from those in control texts and the Greek New Testament.

The Greek NT (The Majority text, very close to what The King James Version translators used) shows an average of 1.69.

Any Z score less than 2.0 is considered statistically insignificant.

A Z score 3.0 or greater is considered highly significant, especially when it represents the average of a high volume of data, as this does. The Peshitta data amounts to several hundred thousand entropy and chi squared scores.

Each Peshitta search is simultaneously accompanied by a control search as well.

The Greek texts are longer than Aramaic, so the skip rates go higher than those of the Peshitta.

Divine Contact-The Original New Testament Discovered

This is because Aramaic , like Hebrew, is a more compact language than western, non-Semitic languages, like Greek.

The Greek data amounts to half a million data, easily.

This amount of data will yield very reliable statistics , which Codecracker itself calculates.

In my early Divine Names Experiments, I searched for ELS's of 84 Divine Names in Hebrew & Aramaic, as written in The Hebrew OT and in the Aramaic of **The Peshitta NT**. These involved a total of 710 Peshitta ELS searches and 758 Control searches. **Z Score avgs. are 3.35 & 3.97** for two refined methods of searching **The Peshitta**.

Controls have **Z Score avgs. 1.51 & 0.94**.

Z Scores of 0.00 – 1.99 are considered normal; **3.0** & greater is high, representing a probability **less than 0.001 for one average word search**.

The searches were done as toroidal searches, with "search wrap on", as only CodeFinder can do, making the search text a cylinder, or circular string with the end of the text connected to the beginning. This eliminates error in the calculation of expected numbers of hits in ELS's of extremely high skip rates. It also normalizes control results at these high skip rates.

A Z Score is calculated by subtracting the expected number (CodeFinder calculates this based on letter frequencies in a text) from the actual number of occurrences. The difference is then divided by the square root of the expected number.

Total probability for the text represented by an avg. Z of 3.0 per ELS would be 0.001 to the 71 billionth power for four letter words, using the formula to calculate the number of ELS's:

$$N = (i - 1)\{2L - (W - 1)(i + 2)\}$$

$N = (i - 1)\{2L - (w - 1)(i + 2)\}$; "i" is the maximum search interval (153,698) ; L is length of text in letters (461,094); w is word length (4), hence N= (153698-1)*((2*461094)-(3*153700))

I present these data and statistics as evidence which controverts Randy Ingermanson's conclusion as stated in the aforementioned book, that no significant number of codes exist in The Bible. His text searches, aside from testing only individual books, cover only 0.060% of the possible searches of The NT as a whole (He tested **The Greek NT**) and only 0.020% of The Hebrew OT. He tested less than 0.10 % of the skip texts , all at the lower end of the scale, and yet he claims this is a scientific endeavor which invalidates Bible codes !

Even testing individual books, like Genesis- using only skips 1 to 150 is only 0.40 % of the possible data to be tested for three letter words (Trigrams)! Digrams occur in greater numbers by a factor of two , therefore, Randy's data represent only 0.20 % of possible Digram skip texts data.

My original experiment to test The Bible systematically for codes in 2002 was to search for Divine names and titles as codes by skipping letters , using a computer program, from 2 letter skips to 461,000 letter skips in The Aramaic NT. The results were phenomenal and staggering !

After using Randy's Codecracker software, which he designed and provided free to his book customers, I found extraordinary results in **The Hebrew OT** and in **The Aramaic NT** (called **The Peshitta**). His program seemed to have bugs in it that made it unreliable, so I pretty much left it alone.

I have recently experimented more with it and have become more adept at using it and realizing its limitations. Randy has a website where one can obtain Codecracker free of charge with The Hebrew OT and Greek NT searchable texts.. I am now convinced that his program validates my results from The Hebrew OT and **The Peshitta NT** using Codefinder, from Kevin Acres at Research Systems Inc.

Divine Contact-The Original New Testament Discovered

I have done extensive searches on the Torah and NT , testing individual books with both programs as well as The Torah as a unit and The NT as a unit. Every test so far reveals an extraordinary phenomenon in both Testaments. These books constituting The Bible, in the original Hebrew and Aramaic (OT & NT !) contain inordinate numbers of **ELS**'s (**E**quidistant **L**etter **S**equences) as compared to non-inspired books, which I have also tested alongside of every Bible search.

The Divine Name experiment validates the hypothesis I set up at the outset, that if God were to put codes in The Bible, He would code it with His Divine Names and Titles, as found throughout The straight Hebrew and Aramaic texts of The Old and New Testaments. I have tested at least 84 of these so far , with highly significant results.

English Bibles do not reveal significant results; **The Greek NT** texts (I have tested three) do not show significant results overall; **War & Peace** in Hebrew does not show significant results.

The only books that show significant results are **The Hebrew - Aramaic Old Testament** and **The Aramaic Peshitta NT**.

CodeCracker and Codefinder give very similar results for an average search: *The avg. ELS has a probability of under 1 in a thousand* .

If you calculate *all the possible four letter ELS's in Matthew's Aramaic*, there are (# letters-max skip-1)*(2* text length)-(3*max skip), or (57798-19265)*((2*57798)-(3*19268)) , or 1.11 billion !

Raising 0.001 to the billionth power- well, that's a ridiculous idea, and
a very, very, very, small chance !

That is effectively a zero chance that Matthew's Gospel was not deliberately coded exactly it is in The Peshitta, with hundreds of thousands of occurrences of at least 95 divine Names and titles as well as an abundance of other coded information.

Looking at this from the other end, that is a
99.99999999999999999999999999999999999999999999999999999999999999999999999999999999999
to the 1,100,000,000[th] place...% well , that would be over a billion decimal places %, that Matthew in The Peshitta is coded deliberately.

Actually, I would round that off to a 100 % chance.
Due to bugs in Codecracker, (its still in its 1.0 version), I have relied on the Trigram Chi Squared Test for analysis. I have found the other tests somewhat erratic for high skip search #'s.

Some will no doubt reply, "No text of the Bible is that precisely preserved so as to retain the exact original wording." Those who so respond are unaware of the precision with which this text was copied, so I will relate some interesting data I have come upon while analyzing **The Peshitta NT** via computer; *This is what makes these kinds of discoveries possible today, and I am amazed so few seem to have taken advantage of computer power to do so.*
The following are early results obtained by using Randy Ingermanson's Codecracker software.

The Greek Textus Receptus , Westcott & Hort''s Greek NT, and Weymouth's NT
served as control texts and produced insignificant results. The KJV Torah was used for
a control in The Torah experiment.
*The following averages are for **Trigram** (3 letter word) **Chi-Squared** searches with CodeCracker 1.0,*
designed by Randy Ingermanson.This seems the most reliable test to use. Digrams have twice the room for error
that Trigrams have.Digram results at high skips are often erratic, even for controls.

The stats below demonstrate the results of 8000 +
searches of over 8000 skip texts. The avg. Z Score of these is **3.60**.
A Z Score of **3.0** represents a probability of one in a thousand.
3.60 represents 1 out of 5000.
This is the text I used for my experiment with <u>CodeFinder 1.22</u>
in my search of 84 Divine Names as codes in <u>The Peshitta NT</u>.
That text has 461,094 letters.
This text differs from two other Peshitta texts by only 50-65 letters,
yet the results are significantly different.

**The Online Bible version of The 1905 Syriac NT
has 461,047 letters. The Avg. Z is 3.25.**

From all I can ascertain, the 2 Western Peshitta texts
are based on the same 1905 Syriac Peshitta , which is a
famous critical edition based on several critical works,
,especially Pusey & Gwilliams 1901 ed. Of The Gospels,
using 41 ancient Eastern & Western Aramaic mss.
The Western Peshitta text avg. *3.42*
The Eastern Peshitta avg. :   *1.81*
The 3 NT control texts avg. :   *1.38*
The KJV NT has an overall Z Score of 1.81
for 9,000 searches.
The English Weymouth NT has an overall Z of 1.73
for 9,000 searches.
The Greek Textus Receptus has a 0.86 Avg. Z for
1,000 searches .

Westcott & Hort's Edition of <u>The Greek NT</u> has
a 1.87 Z Score Avg for 1,000 searches.

The Greek Byzantine NT has a 0.26 Avg. Z for 1000
searches.

The KJV NT has an Avg. Z of 1.81 for 9000 searches.
Herman Melville's Moby Dick has an
overall Z Score of 1.78 (5,000 searches).
The Eastern Peshitta (NT canon has 22 books) has an
overall Z Score of 1.81 (2,000 searches).
(A Z score less than 2.0 is not considered statistically significant.)
These results using CodeCracker 1.0 seem to confirm
the Divine Names experiment results qualitatively and
quantitatively.
The Divine Names experiment yields Z Score avgs. of 3.14 – 4.73.
This Codecracker experiment gives 3.05 – 4.0 avgs.
The controls for each avg. 0.13 – 1.55 & 1.28 – 1.87 , resp.

The Eastern Peshitta (NT canon has 22 books) has an
ancient tradition according to The Church of The East as being
the original New Testament text as written by the Apostles.
It was very carefully copied and preserved by its Eastern scribes
with a written Massorah which preserves the precise readings
and statistics of the original text, as The Hebrew Massorah
did for Old Testament Hebrew scribes.
Its manuscripts are a monument to careful devotion in
scribal skill, since they contain almost no errors to speak of,
in comparison to each other and The Critical Edition employed in
these experiment. One manuscript I have info. on differs only 8 times
from the critical text edition in Paul's Epistles.
That amounts to approx. 1 difference per every 10 pages !

There is no such tradition associated with the Greek NT
or any other NT text, nor such agreement among manuscripts.

Discounting the 12 verses of John 7:53-8:11,The Eastern and Western Peshittas differ
in The Gospels and Acts by only 95 letters ! That is a nearly miraculous phenomenon.
The mss. range from early 5th century to the 8th century.

It stands to reason that with such accurate mss and scribal
tradition behind the two Peshitta versions, a critical collation
of a good number of them should produce a near perfect , if not perfect,
edition of The first New Testament !

The two Western editions I have tested here differ from each other by only
a total of 50 letters throughout the entire NT !
The version I received for CodeFinder 1.22 and which I
used in the original experiment contains 461,094 letters.
50 letters amounts to 1 ten thousandth of the NT.
That is 99.99% agreement !

The Greek NT Textus Receptus exists in various editions, whose
mss. are the most consistent and carefully copied of all Greek
mss. Elzevir's 1633 edition differs from Robert Stephens 1550
edition by about 87 letters in 1 Corinthians !
That , while only 2 thousandths of the book's 33,260 letters,
is still twenty times the variation found in the Western Peshitta editions.

The modern Critical Editions of The Greek NT have much wider
divergences; ten times greater than those of The Elzevir and Stephens Editions of The
Textus Receptus.

The Codecracker test of <u>The Hebrew Torah shows an Avg. Z Score of 3.17</u> **, based on 4500 skip texts and 4500 randomized texts.**

The KJV shows an Avg. Z Score of 0.93. Using a 1.0 for control purposes,
The Torah cumulative probability for 5000 skip texts would be $10^{-15,000}$!
The book of Genesis would yield a probability of $10^{-230,000}$!

The Aramaic Peshitta NT shows an Avg. Z Score of 3.42 , based on 2,000 skip texts
(not including 2,000 randomized skip texts).
The Controls shows an Avg. Z Score of 1.78.
A Z Score of 3.42 is roughly representative of a probability 0.0003.
A Z of 1.78, rounded to 2.0 is roughly a 0.02 probability.
Subtracting the log of the latter from the log of the former gives 2×10^{-2},
or 0.02 for an average **relative** probability per skip text.
(The relative probability is not the actual average result; it is modified downward by dividing the control result into the Peshitta result. I whipped this method up on my own, and don't believe it is a standard practice in statistics. I do not use this method in my later analysis.)
10,000 skip texts would have a probablity 1E-17,000, or $10^{-17,000}$.
That is a small part of one book's potential skip texts !

I wouldn't care to compute the chances for The four Gospel's codes,
much less the whole New Testament .

The relative probabilities for Torah and Peshitta texts are very close to each other !
The Torah's is 0.0100; The Peshitta's is 0.009.
This is an amazing development, n'est ce pas ?

About 48% of the 5000 X^2 Z Scores for skip bands 500-5000 in The Hebrew Torah are > 4.0;
About 47% of the 5000 X^2 Z Scores for The Peshitta are > 4.0.

Codefinder Peshitta (461,094 letters)

Z's > 5.0	28.89%
Count	180.00
Overall Z (Trigrams) 3.31	
Overall % Z > 4	51.89%

OLB Jacobite(461,047 Lttrs)

Z's > 5.0	44.69%
Overall Z	3.07

Trigram X^2
<u>Eastern Peshitta</u>

Cum. Avg. Z	2.24
Count	180
Avg. Z Score	3.8
Median Z	4.04
Z's > 5.0	14.44%
10,000 Di&Trichi	1.64
Indiv. Avg. Z	0.69
Overall Z (Trigrams)	1.81

Trigram X^2
<u>The Greek NT</u>:

The Greek Textus Receptus has a **0.86** Avg. Z for 1,000 searches .

Westcott & Hort's Edition of <u>The Greek NT</u> has a **1.87** Z Score Avg for 1,000 searches.

The Greek Byzantine NT has a **0.26** Avg. Z for 1000 searches.
That is a 1.59 Average for The three Greek texts. All of the control scores are within the normal range for random results.

These results are simply confirmation of previous results I achieved using CodeFinder 1.22 and MS Excel. I don't rely on these Codecracker results for my position on the Bible codes. It is interesting however, that my use of Randy Ingermanson's program, CodeCracker, has seemed to turn his conclusion about Bible codes on its head !

His book ,**<u>Who Wrote The Bible Code ?</u>**, is based on much too small a sampling of the data of the Hebrew Bible to conclude anything; he also ignores Aramaic altogether in his testing (also very small data samples) of The NT.

Chapter 14- Verifying the Results -Aramaic or Greek : Will the real original please stand up ?

(Don't be put off by the seeming complexity of this chapter; simply look for the higher percentage figures in the primacy numbers in the comparisons of the Greek and Aramaic texts in the tables below.)
The following chapters consist of data from some of eight comprehensive studies I have performed which support my original hypothesis in this way: If the Peshitta is Divinely written and coded and the Greek NT is not, The Peshitta has been sanctioned as the original New Testament and the Greek would be derived from The original, and would not be the original itself. The data in the following studies strongly support the primacy (originality) of The Peshitta NT in its Western form (All 27 books) and also support strongly that The Greek NT, in all of its forms, is a translation of that Peshitta NT.

A Computerized Primacy Test of The Byzantine NT , Westcott & Hort Greek NT and The Peshitta NT.

By Glenn David Bauscher

Abstract:

A computerized analysis of Aramaic & Greek cognates in The Peshitta and Byzantine New Testaments reveals a dramatic role reversal in the relationship assigned these two texts by Western textual critics. This may prove the most radical discovery ever in the "science" of Bible Textual Criticism. I use the word "science" advisedly here, as most of what is called Textual Criticism , if not all, completely ignores the scientific method in arriving at its conclusions about the origins and text of the New Testament. This paper presents the basis and results of an experiment that tests the two major Greek NT texts – The Critical Text of Westcott & Hort-1881, based on the two oldest NT uncial mss. ,Vaticanus & Sinaiticus,and the Byzantine Greek Majority Textform 1991 edition of Maurice Robinson versus The Peshitta NT (the combined critical editions of Gwilliams & Pusey, Gwynn and Pinkerton, used in The UBS 1979 Syriac NT ,also known as the 1905 Syriac NT) to ascertain which is the translation and which is the original behind that translation. The 15,000 data produced support the unconventional conclusion that both Greek texts are translations of The Peshitta NT text.

I have employed the scientific method in an experiment described in this article. I have studied Biology, Physics,Organic Chemistry, Calculus, Cell Physiology, Genetics,Evolution, etc., as a Pre-Med student at Rutgers University until the middle of my Junior year, when I changed majors and transferred to another university to study Theology and The Greek NT. There I received a B.A. in Pastoral Studies with a minor in Biology. I have also taught Science and Math at the high school level, so I have enough background to write and speak knowledgeably and confidently on the subject of science and the scientific method.

Divine Contact-The Original New Testament Discovered

*I am an ordained minister since 1976.My passion of thirty years has been studying and teaching the Hebrew and Greek Bibles, and Textual Criticism ,particularly of the NT. During the past four years I have been studying Aramaic and **The Peshitta NT**. I have written several articles for BibleCodeDigest.com's newsletter during that time about The Peshitta N.T.research I have been doing.*

*I was also part of the translation team for Peshitta.org's **Interlinear Peshitta NT** project, headed up by Paul Younan.I have translated The four Gospels from Aramaic to English in a word for word Interlinear thus far.*

I intend to finish The New Testament within a year or so.

The Scientific Method:

- I. *State an hypothesis.*
- II. *Test it by experiment.*
- III. *Observe and record results.*
- IV. *If results support the hypothesis sufficiently, state the theory.*
- V. *Continue testing the theory.*
- VI. *If theory is irrefutable over sufficient time, state The Law.*

Below are Aramaic & Greek word comparisons in the Peshitta N.T.and The Byzantine Greek NT-
 (some Westcott & Hort Greek N.T.comparisons as well).

These have a pattern, which compares very well with 11 Hebrew-LXX Greek studies also presented here- The Peshitta matches Hebrew word results and The Greek N.T.matches LXX results, which we know was translated from the Hebrew OT.

Suffice it here to say the higher percentage results for each two word pair comparisons will determine the original text.

Hebrew/Greek ratios are higher than Greek/Hebrew ratios; Hebrew/Greek ratios represent the Hebrew O.T. original-LXX translation model.

The Greek/Hebrew ratios represent an hypothetical LXX original- Hebrew translation model; it is always lower than the Hebrew/Greek ratios.

(These ratios are not mere comparisons of totals; for example:

They compare the total # of occurrences of a Greek word with the number of times its Hebrew counterpart is found in the same grammatical place in the parallel Hebrew verse; this is a correlation ratio. This will be done for both languages for each word pair- Hebrew/Greek & Greek/Hebrew.

Of course, The N.T.studies are concerned with Aramaic/Greek & Greek/Aramaic.

These correspond with the O.T. results, showing that The Peshitta fits the pattern of an original and the Greek N.T.fits the role of a translation.

It's all in the numbers!

I will illustrate the process of analyzing two texts, one of which is a translation of the other, to determine which is the original and which is the translation.

Divine Contact-The Original New Testament Discovered

If one has two flasks of clear liquid, one of which we know was distilled from the other, how can we determine which is the original undistilled solution and which is the distillate?

If the original is alcohol and water and the distillate is pure alcohol, how shall we determine which is which? We can test boiling points, density, freezing points, dissolution, etc., and determine contents and percentage of purity for each liquid. If we find one flask is 75 % water and 25 % Ethyl Alcohol and the other contains 99.99 % Ethyl Alcohol, and we know that one is distilled from solution taken from the other flask, how difficult would it be to determine that the 99.99 % solution came from solution taken from the other 75 % flask?

It should be just as easy to determine the original text between The Greek text (whether Critical,Byzantine,Western, or Caesarean) and The Peshitta. ***Conventional wisdom has it that The Peshitta is a translation of <u>The Greek NT</u>, circa the early 5th century A.D. The Greek texts are supposed to represent the original New Testament text.***

The following data represents an analysis of the contents of two "flasks", one of which was "distilled" from the contents represented in the other "flask". A ratio will be derived for each one and a determination made as to which is the original "solution". Do not confuse the distillate with the original; the original will actually be represented by a lower percentage concentration than the translation. I will explain this later.

Every good science experiment will employ a control subject- a comparison against a known quantity that should produce insignificant and predictable results. In this experiment I chose to test The LXX and Hebrew O.T. as a control model. *(The LXX is The Septuagint Greek translation of The Hebrew Bible.It was produced around 285 B.C., commissioned by King Ptolemy of Egypt.)*

Before choosing a control, I developed a hypothesis and a methodology for testing it.

I chose a cognate word pair from Greek and Aramaic (one word in each of the two languages , both meaning essentially the same thing).Example: Greek (πνευμα- "pneuma",meaning "spirit", "wind", "breath"), and Aramaic רוחא- "rukha", meaning "spirit", "wind", "breath").

I. The Hypothesis:

I hypothesized that the total # of the translation words should be smaller than the total for its cognate original. This would be due to missed occurrences of an original word or failure to translate it in some places; another more likely reason is that there may be another possible translation than the common cognate word, hence the total # of the translation word is <u>generally</u> smaller than that of the original.

Much more important than the totals , however, is the ratio of the number of <u>correlating original words</u> to <u>the total number of the translation cognate word</u> in the text. *Normally* these words must exceed 100 each in total number for the statistics to be significant. This ratio will exceed the ratio <u>of the number of correlated translated words</u> to <u>the total number of the original words</u>.

One must calculate the total for each word and a correlation number for its corresponding cognate, then find and compare the respective ratios. A control like the Hebrew O.T. –LXX model, which is a known quantity, the LXX being a translation of The Hebrew OT, shows a pattern for these word pair studies. The pattern of this model fits the hypothesis proposed above.

To determine this, I needed to see all verses with a searched word in Greek with all those same verses listed in Aramaic in parallel fashion, verse by verse.[This I did with Online Bible Millenium Edition and pasted all verses into MS Word, where I did further searches with the "find" feature, which provides number of hits for a search word.]

Why did I expect the above ratio statement to be true ? It is tied to the logic behind the distillation illustration – ("**The Still**").

Every molecule of alcohol in the distilled flask came from the original solution; not so for the reversed proposition. Therefore the ratio of alcohol content in the original to alcohol content in the distilled flask will be greater (due to inefficiency of the evaporation-condensation process) than the ratio of distilled alcohol volume to the total original solution. I explain how I applied this analogy to the Bible versions below.

Divine Contact-The Original New Testament Discovered

The translation process is a distillation or filtering process whereby the original words are sifted through a translator and converted into something equivalent but different and generally smaller in overall volume (some is "lost in translation").Hence, the volume and concentration ratios will differ in the ways described above.

Simply put, the distilled version is not the original and is easily distinguished from it.

Another matter I must address is the choice of texts and the objection that we don't know that we have the original or anything close enough to the original to do a reliable comparison and analysis.

I have found that the results vary very little if at all between text types for most word studies. The Westcott & Hort Edition of the Greek N.T.yields results practically identical to the Byzantine Greek text in all N.T.word searches I have done for these two editions. The reason is simple: All major text types agree in approx. 97% of the N.T.text. All the controversy that has arisen concerning the N.T.text is raging over 3 % of the text !

Example: the οι dipthong –(omicron, iota combination) occurs 7766 times in Westcott & Hort's Ed. In the Byzantine text, it occurs 7928 times. That is 98% agreement. The masculine nominative singular article ο- "ha"occurs 3146 times in W&H; 3313 in The Byzantine Majority text. That is 95% agreement.

This means that it is irrelevant which Greek text is chosen; the results will be the same. The particle δε – "but"occurs 2763 times in W&H and 2844 times in the 1991 Robinson-Pierpoint Byzantine edition. That is 97% agreement. One more: The preposition υπο – ("under", "by") occurs 427 times in W&H; 442 in Byz.That is 96.5% agreement. These examples were randomly chosen in the order presented with no omissions.

The Westcott & Hort Greek NT is basically the type text behind most modern English versions of The New Testament- The NIV,The Living Bible, New Living Translation, NASV, Revised Version, New Revised Version. The Byzantine Greek is essentially the same as the Greek edition used by The King James translators for the New Testament and is also represented by The New King James Version.

II. The Procedure:

Normally a translation may be discerned as such by choosing a word pair (Aramaic, Greek) or Hebrew , LXX Greek)and analyzing it, for example: (ארעא, γη) ; both mean, "earth", "land".

This is how it works:

Do a total search for all occurrences of a particular Greek word- γη,

for example. (I use Online Bible 1.42 with LXX, Hebrew BHS, Byzantine Greek, Westcott & Hort Greek NT, TR 1550, Peshitta 1905 NT, Latin Vulgate, Murdock's Translation, etc.).

The OLB can list all versions for each verse in parallel fashion and do multiple simultaneous searches and give a count for # of verses containing a search word or phrase. Boolean searches can also be done with wildcards, thus all words with a root "γη"can be searched simultaneously by searching for "γη*".

The results can be saved to clipboard and and pasted to MS WORD and further analyzed for word #'s .

I would do this search in OLB 1.42 with the Byzantine Greek as the search text and Peshitta opened as an alternate version below the Greek.

I would also search The Peshitta N.T.for the related & parallel Aramaic roots found in the first search, in the same fashion described above, making sure all words with the same root are found : ארעא can be found by searching , "*ארע*" .

This latter search has the Byzantine Greek N.T.opened below The Peshitta as an alternate version. All the verses are pasted into MS Word and analyzed as before, counting numbers of Aramaic search words and corresponding Greek words that match up with the corresponding Aramaic word in the same verse.

Example:

Mt 2:6 (**Byzantine Greek**) και συ βηθλεεμ γη ιουδα ουδαμως ελαχιστη ει εν τοις ηγεμοσιν ιουδα εκ σου γαρ εξελευσεται ηγουμενος οστις ποιμανει τον λαον μου τον ισραηλ

Divine Contact-The Original New Testament Discovered

אנתי בית-לחם דיהודא לא הויתי בצירא במלכא דיהודא מנכי גיר נפוק מלכא דהו נרעיוהי לעמי איסראיל
אף (Peshitta Aramaic) Mt 2:6

Mt 2:6 And thou Bethlehem, [in] the land of Juda, art not the least among the princes of Juda: for out of thee shall come a Governor, that shall rule my people Israel.

Mt 4:15 (**Byzantine Greek**) γη ζαβουλων και γη νεφθαλειμ οδον θαλασσης περαν του ιορδανου γαλιλαια των εθνων

ארעא דזבולון ארעא דנפתלי אורחא דימא עברוהי דיורדנן גלילא דעממא (Peshitta Aramaic) Mt 4:15

Mt 4:15 The land of Zabulon, and the land of Nephthalim, [by] the way of the sea, beyond Jordan, Galilee of the Gentiles;

Mt 5:18 (**Byzantine Greek**) αμην γαρ λεγω υμιν εως αν παρελθη ο ουρανος και η γη ιωτα εν η μια κεραια ου μη παρελθη απο του νομου εως αν παντα γενηται

אמר אנא לכון דעדמא דנעברון שמיא וארעא יוד חד סרטא לא נעבר מן נמוסא עדמא דכל נהוא
אמין גיר (Peshitta Aramaic) Mt 5:18

Mt 5:18 For verily I say unto you, Till heaven and earth pass, one jot or one tittle shall in no wise pass from the law, till all be fulfilled.

These are just the first three verses of the results for a search for the Greek word for "**earth**"- γη (pronounced "gay" in the Byzantine Greek NT.
The Peshitta Aramaic verse is shown below the Greek verse; The Aramaic word for "earth" - ארעא (pronounced "Aara", is highlighted blue, as is the Greek word for earth ,γη. The King James Version is below that.

The Greek search in OLB will give all occurrences of γη in the NT;
It will also list all the verses containing this Greek word in as many versions as I have opened. I have <u>The Peshitta</u> opened as well, so every verse listed in Greek will have the same verse below it in <u>The Peshitta</u>'s Aramaic (Hebrew fonts –OLBHEB are used).
When I have counted the Greek and Aramaic words in this file , using MS Word's Edit – Find feature, I can obtain the ratio of number of corresponding Aramaic words divided by the number of the searched Greek root.
In this example, γη* occurs <u>251 times</u>, <u>meaning</u> γη (meaning,"earth", "land") occurs 251times, The Peshitta has ארעא ("Earth","land") 242 times.
One must be very clear that the second number, **<u>242, is not a simple total of the occurrences of ארעא in The Peshitta</u>**. It is *<u>the number of</u> grammatically correlated occurrences* of ארעא ("Earth") to the 251 occurrences of γη ("Earth") in all those sentences where ארעא occurs.
Divide the Greek # into the Aramaic#: **Aramaic/Greek , or 242/251 = 96.41%.**
This ratio normally will give the percentage of Greek words that are matched up with the Aramaic root words ! <u>This will represent the Aramaic Primacy number!</u> It is also a concentration number, consistent with the stillery example above.
The reverse search of total Aramaic words in <u>The Peshitta</u> is done separately on Online Bible, with Greek listed as an alternate version beneath <u>the Peshitta</u> , & must be pasted (making sure all verses in OLB are copied into MS Word) and analyzed as the first search file. This time the number of occurrences of the searched Aramaic word is counted and divided by the number of occurrences of the corresponding Greek word.
All Aramaic searches can be done simultaneously with boolean searches: We want now to search total number of ארעא in The Peshitta: This would be entered as *ארע* to include all ארע's with proclitics and enclitics (prefixes and suffixes).

Divine Contact-The Original New Testament Discovered

There are **286 total** occurrences of ארעא in all forms in **The Peshitta NT**.

The Byzantine Greek was opened as alternate version below The Peshitta while the search was done. Both versions are displayed for all the search results, verse by verse.

There will often be references that will have to be deleted, since they will contain unwanted Aramaic or Greek words .

MS WORD shows that γη occurs **246 times** as a corresponding word to ארעא.

Now divide the Aramaic # into the Greek #: **Greek/Aramaic** , or **246/286 = 86.01%.**

This ratio will represent the percentage of Aramaic words that are matched up with the corresponding Greek word(s).

I will call this the Greek Primacy Score.

It looks like the Peshitta is the original and The Byzantine Greek N.T. is the translation- 96% to 86%.

96 % Ethyl alcohol would be 192 proof ! That's pretty strong "proof" !

So far, every word pair studied ,out of 22 examples,gives a Aramaic Primacy score (concentration of Aramaic to Greek) that is higher than the Greek score.

This method is consistent for simple and straightforward word pairs. The LXX and Hebrew O.T. show consistent results for 11 word pairs totaling over 2600 words found in The LXX and 2300 in The Hebrew Tanach.

The Peshitta yields consistent results for 22 word pairs, totaling 4215 Aramaic words as compared to The Byzantine Greek N.T., totaling 3826 words in 22 tests of 22 word pair searches. **The Peshitta-Greek %'s are : 90.75 % to 77.00 %**

The Hebrew OT-LXX %'s are: **86.71 % to 66.12 %.** These numbers are not absolute scores or probabilities-merely relative indicators showing that the text with the higher score is most likely to be the base text ,of which the other is most likely a translation.

I believe this is a conclusive method of determining which of two versions, known to be related as an **original & translation** pair, is the translation and which is the original. I find it hard to believe no none has ever discovered this before and applied it to the Greek N.T.and Peshitta versions. The same method works for The Latin Vulgate and Greek NT's.

Another very interesting result is that the Catholic Epistles and Revelation of Gwynn's Peshitta Edition also appear to be the original behind Westcott & Hort's Greek text of the same. This would seem to validate the 27 book Western canon in its entirety as a very early Aramaic text of which the known Greek texts, with mss. dating back to the second century, are all translations.

III. The Results:

Here are the actual results in table form:

The Percentages on the right are consistently higher , indicating the Peshitta Primacy Score.

Jacobite Peshitta searches vs. aligned Greek NT:Greek NT searches vs. aligned Jacobite Peshitta :	
Greek Primacy numbers	**Peshitta Primacy numbers**
Search for total # Aramaic word *Greek/Aramaic % Aramaic Greek words*	**Search for total # Greek word** *Aramaic/Greek % Greek Aram words*
divided into # corresp. Greek words	**divided into # corresp. Aramaic words**
("Demon")	*("Demon")*
דיונא,דיוא-39	δαιμονιον, δαιμονιζομαι-

78

שאדא-48 | | | | | | דיון-8

1. דיוא-30

Δαιμονιον, δαιμονιζομαι- 79 | | | | שאדא-40

79/87= 91% | | 90.80% | | 87 79 | 100.00% | 78 78

78/78=100%

("Spirit") | | | ("Spirit")

רוחא = 498 times in The Peshitta NT : Πνευμα occurs 413 times in The Byz.Greek NT.

;of these , The Greek version has the following parallels: רוח parallels these 404 times in The Peshitta NT.

πνευμα = 401 ; 401/498 = 80.52% 498 401 404/413=97.82% 413 404

ανεμος = 31 (This represents the Peshitta base-Greek translation model of the NT.)

μακροθυμεω = 25

απολογεω = 18

πνεω , πνευστος = 7 (See 2 Tim. 3:16)

totals 482

("Satan") | | | ("Satan")

14 times out of 40, the Aramaic, "Satana", "סטנא", is translated, Διαβολος-38

"διαβολος"; once "אכלקרצא" is translated, "σατανας". אכלקרצא-16

26 times out of 40, the Aramaic, "Satana", "סטנא", is translated, "σατανας".

סטנא-16 35.00% 40 14 | | 42.11% | 38 16

Greek Primacy numbers | **Peshitta Primacy numbers**

מרן-323 ("Lord") | | | κυριος- 263 ("Lord")

Κυριος-304 | | | מר root – 254

304/323 = 93% | 94.12% 323 | 304 | 97% of κυριος 96.58% 263 | 254

are correlated to מר -,(מרה,מרד,מרא,מרי,מרן,מריא).

ארע – 288 ("Earth") | 86.11% | 288 248 γη- 251 96.41% 251 ("Earth") 242

γη – 246 (parallels to ארע) –Two are unconnected to ארע. | ארע – 242

οικουμενη – 9 | | | 242/251 = 96% for ארע

/γη

χωρα – 6

επιγειος – 2

248/288= 86% for γη / ארע

("To","With") | | | ("To","With")

לות occurs 72 times in The Peshitta from Mat. 1:1-Mark 2:13 & in those places προς,παρα occur-71

 correspond to לות; 71/72=99%

69 cases of parallel עד, לות

98.61% 72 71 | | 69 total cases of προς ; 69/69 = 100.00% 69 69

("give an answer", "make a defense") | | ("give an answer", "make a defense")

מפק ברוח = 17 | | | απολογεομαι,απολογια = 19

απολογ- = 13

מפק רוה = 17 times				
13/17= 76% 19 **17**	**76.47%**	17	**13**	17/19 = 89% **89.47%**
("To","With")		("To","With")		
לות- 314				Προς- 362
προς- 194				לות- 251
194/314 = 62% **251**	**61.78%** 314 **194**	251/362= 69% for Aramaic 69.34%		362
62% for Greek original				
("Word")		("Word")		
מלת -378		Λογο(ς,υ,ω,ν) , ρημα occurs 324 times		
Λογος, ρημα -336		מלא occurs 308 times		
336/378 = **88.90%** 336 378			**95.00%** 324 308	
95% of λογος, ρημα are paralleled by מלא				
Greek Primacy numbers		**Peshitta Primacy numbers**		
("Book","writing", "scribe")		("Book","writing", "scribe")		
ספר(א)-99				βιβλος-46
כתב-200 147				γραμματευς, γραμμα-
כתבא-97				γραφη-25
2. 218				
Βιβλος-46				כתבא-53
Γραφη-47				ספרא-132
Γραμματευς, γραμμα,-71				185
164				
164//396=41% **41.41%** 396 164			185/218=85% **84.86%** 218 185	
("Beginning","Head","First")		("Beginning","Head","First")		
Only 43% of total # ראש are associated with αρχη.				αρχη-50
רשית-14				
רישית-3				
רשא-7				
42.99% 107 **46**		24/50 =48%	**48.00%** 50 **24**	
("Messiah","Anointed","Christ")		("Messiah","Anointed","Christ")		
משיח-165				Χριστος-157
Χριστος- 150				משיח-149
150/165 =91%	**90.91%** 165 **150**	149/157 = 95%	**94.90%** 157 **149**	

Luke & Acts

Here is an amazing demonstration of the originality of The Peshitta text and the Greek N.T.as a translation of
The Aramaic Peshitta. The Peshitta has ישוע 246 times , 82 times more than The Greek text of Luke & Acts !
Ιησους occurs 164 times in all its forms in The Majority Text of Greek Luke and Acts.
158 of these are paralleled by the Aramaic ישוע in The Peshitta of Luke & Acts.- 96% correspondence!

("Jesus")		("Jesus")			
Ιησου- 164					
Ιησου- 155					ישוע -158
155/246=63% 246 155		158/164= 96%	**96.34%**	164	**158**
In Luke					**In Luke**
ישוע-175					Ιησους-98
ιησους-84					ישוע-97
Vulgate-Iesus- 88					
KJV-Jesus-96					ישוע / Ιησους = 98%
84/175=55% **48.0%** 174 84			**97.7%**	88	86

Whole NT		**In NT**	
("Peace,greeting")		**("Peace,greeting")**	
שלמא-145		ασπαζομαι-70	
שינא-3		שלמא - 71	
100% of Greek terms are paralleled by The Aramaic equivalent.			
Ειρηνη-83		ειρηνη-100	
Ασπαζομαι-52		שלמא-85	
Χαιρε-1		שינא-13	
135/148 **91.22%** 148 135	98/100 = 98%;	**98.00%** 100 98	

91.22% of Aramaic terms are paralleled by The Greek equivalent.

Greek Primacy numbers	**Peshitta Primacy numbers**
("I AM", "I am")	**("I am")**
אנא אנא-48 times	εγω ειμι-45
εγω ειμι-38 times	
אנא אנא-39	

36/45 = 80% of Greek terms are paralleled by The Aramaic equivalent

38/48= 79%	**79.17%** 48 38	**80.00%** 45 36

אנא אנא would not be a likely translation of the Greek εγω ειμι;

אנא is far more likely as a translation of Greek "εγω ειμι".

("Love")		("Love")
חוב-340		αγαπαω,-η-320

αγαπαω,-η-294				חוב-282
294/340=86%	86.47% 340	294		282/320= 88.13% 320
282				

("Life")				**("Life")**
חיין,חיא-224				ζωη-135
ζωη-169				חיין,חיא-135
169/224=75%	75.45% 224 169			135/135= 100.00% 135
135				
("World", Age")				**("World", Age")**
עלם,עלמא-413				αιων-198
αιων-195				κοσμος-205
κοσμος-184				עלם,עלמא-402
379/413=92%	91.77% 413 379			400/403= 99.26% 403 400

Greek Primacy numbers   **Peshitta Primacy numbers**

("Righteous,(ness)", "Good,(ness)", "Alms")			**("Righteous,(ness)", "Good,(ness)", "Alms")**	
זדיק, זדק - 88 + 53 = 141 δικαιοσυνη-218			δικαιοω, δικαιος,	
כאנותא, כאנא – 94			ελεημοσυνη-17	
3. 235				
δικαιος- 184 111			זדיקותא, זדיקתא, זדיקא-	
ελεημοσυνη -14			כאנו כאנותא, כאנא-90	
4. 201				
198/235= 84%	84.26% 235	198	201/235 = 85.53% 235 201	

("Truth", "True", "Truly")			**("Truth", "True", "Truly")**	
שרירא, שרירא – 224				
קושת- 34				
258				
αληθεια,αληθη, αληθινος, αληθειν, etc.- 195			αληθεια and related – 187	
στερεος, στερεωμα, etc. -4			שרירא – 66	
βεβαιος-4			שרדא-86	
ομολογουμενως			קושתא – 30	
οντως-7			182	
αψευδης – 1				
ειπερ -1			182/187= 97%	
γνησιως-4				
195/253 = 77 %	77.08% 253 195		97.33% 187 182	

Avg. for Greek Primacy: Tot. # words	Tot. # words	Avg. for Aramaic Primacy: Tot. # words	Tot. # words
75.8%	4934 **3799**	88.3%	4215 **3826**
22 word pairs analyzed			
Total word # avg.	77.0%	*Avg.*	*Total words* 90.8%

(2.)

The Peshitta in Luke has ישוע *(Jesus) 176 times ,* **78 times more than The Greek text of Luke!**
How can it be ,assuming that a translator with the Greek text before him was translating into the
Aramaic of The Peshitta, added ישוע *("Yeshua"-Jesus) 78 times in Luke alone ?!*
*It is highly unlikely that a translator would be adding words, especially 78 of them-***80% more than**
the text from which he is reading! *It is far more likely that a scribe or translator would omit the Name*
than that he would add it, as omission in translation and copying is a far more common error.The Peshitta
primacy theory requires that **44% of the Aramaic occurrences were dropped** *by a Greek translator-***certainly**
more likely than fabricating 80% more than the original *, if the Aramaic were the translation!*
I challenge anyone to find a similar reverse example as simple and straightforward as this, to demonstrate
the originality of **the Greek NT** *and the Peshitta as its translation.*

(The Peshitta N.T.contains 138 more verses with ישוע *than The Byzantine Greek N.T.has with* Ιησους.*)*
There are no exceptions among these examples.Each shows a higher Peshitta Primacy Score than the Greek
Primacy Score.

(3.)

Consider Mark 5:41,John 1:38,41,42,9:7,Acts 9:36. **The Greek mss. all give a declared translation**
("ερμηνεια",- "hermayneia" *meaning* **"Translation"***-Our English word* **"Hermeneutics"** *derives from this)*
from Aramaic with the transliterated Aramaic first and the Greek translation following.
The Peshitta has none of these in those verses;simply the plain Aramaic. In these places then,
the Greek plainly states that it is a translation of Aramaic, *Israel's native and only tongue for centuries.*
The Peshitta has no such stated translations from Greek into Aramaic.
There are a few translations of Hebrew and perhaps of Palestinian Aramaic into Syrian Aramaic in
Mark's Gospel.

(4.)

Using the Hebrew OT-LXX model (to the right) as a standard , the Peshitta-Greek N.T.results ,based on
almost 10,000 words, support the conclusion that The Greek N.T. as a whole is a translation of **The Peshitta**
NT*.*
The Peshitta – Primacy Score is 90.75% compared to The Greek Score of 77.00 %.

Hebrew O.T. searches vs. aligned LXX:Greek LXX searches vs. aligned Hebrew O.T. :	
Greek LXX Primacy numbers	**Hebrew OT Primacy numbers**
Search for total # Hebrew word	**Greek/Hebrew %** Heb Words Greek words *Search for total # Greek*
word **Heb./Grk %** Grk wds Heb Words	
divided into # corresp. Greek words	*divided into # corresp. Hebrew*
words	
("Spirit")	**("Spirit")**
Total O.T. has 275 Πνευμα **/392** רוח **=70%**	

("Spirit")		("Spirit")	
רוח-392	Πνευμα-275	Πνευμα-307	
Πνευμα-275	**70.15%** 392 275	רוח-278	**90.55%** 307 278

ה שטן, *"Satan"*- 15 places in The Hebrew Bible and the LXX translation of those 15 into "Diabolos":

100.00% 15	15	**100.00%** 15 15	

("LORD")		("Lord")	
In Hebrew OT:		κυριος – 354	
יהוה – 165		יהוה – 256	
In LXX:		אדני, אדון – 80	
κυριος – 148 parallels	336/354= **95% of** κυριος is paralleled by יהוה, אדני, אדון .		
89.70% 165	148	**94.92%** 354 336	
Totals for Heb Gen.		Totals for LXX Genesis & parallel Hebrew OT:	

("Earth","land")		("Earth","land")	
γη – 412			
ארץ – 337		ארץ – 340	
אדמה – 47		אדמה – 48 (assoc. w/γη)	
שדה- 58		שדה – 3	
Γη – 380		391/412 = 95% for	
(שדה,אדמה,ארץ)/γη –Hebrew original & Greek LXX translation of Hebrew			
380/442=**86%** for γη / ארץ + אדמה +שדה **85.97%** 442	380	**94.90%** 412 391	

("Beginning","Head","First")		("Beginning","Head","First")	
ראש- 254		αρχη- 184	
Αρχη-62		ראש – 105	
Κεφαλη- 88		תחל-18	
Πρωτος- 42		שלטן-9	
62/254=24%	**24.41%** 254 62	105/184=**57%** for ראש **57.07%** 184 105	
("Messiah","Anointed", "Christ")		("Messiah","Anointed", "Christ")	

משה, משיח- 120 100			χρισμα, χριστος , χρισειν –

χριστος, χρισμα -94			משה, משיח = 86
94/120= 75%	**78.33%** 120 94	86/100= 86%	**86.00%** 100 86

("I AM", "I am")   **("I am")**

אנכי-174 in Gen-Ruth			εγω ειμι-58
εγω ειμι-58; 58/174 = 33%			אנכי-24
33.33% 174 58		**41.38%** 58 24	

("Love")   **("Love")**

אהב-246			αγαπαω,-η-251
αγαπαω,-η-191			אהב-200
191/246=78%	**77.64%** 246 191	200/251=80%	**79.68%** 251 200

Greek LXX Primacy numbers   **Hebrew OT Primacy numbers**
("World", Age")   **("World", Age")**

עלם,עולם-460 -			αιων-533(-19 redundant)
עד-49			עלם,עולם-439
αιων-497(-19 redundant) = 478			עד-45
478/509 = 94%	**93.91%** 509 478	484/511=95%	**94.72%** 511 484

("Truth", "True", "Truly")   **("Truth", "True", "Truly")**

אמן, אמנה -74	Αληθεια-199

אמת – 179				אמת – 104
5. אמן – 19				
αληθεια-123				אמונת – 27
123/253= 49%	**48.62%** 253	123	150/199 = **75.38%** 199	150
יציב – 4				
קשט – 3				
נכון – 6				
נכח-4				
17				
("Word")				("Word")
דבר-275				λογος-57
אמרת -12				ρημα – 165
287				222
1-λαλεω-107				אמרת – 3
2-ρημα-78				דבר- 274
3-ειπον-88	**34.15%** 287 98	275	**99.55%** 222 221	
4-λογος-23				
5-πραγμα -4 matched by Hebrew דבר.			Just about 100% of Greek terms are	
6 – ερεις-15				
#2+ #4= 98				
98/287= 34%				

Avg for LXX Primacy: Total Words	Total # Words	Total # Words	Avg.for Hebrew Primacy Total Words	
66.9%	2857	1922	83.1%	2613	2290
11 word pairs/groups				
Greek LXX Primacy Score	Hebrew OT Primacy Score			

Total words (Corresp.Hebrew)/Greek	*Total word # avg (Corresp.Greek)/Hebrew*
67.27%	88%

(5.)

The above is research of the Hebrew O.T. and The LXX (Greek Septuagint translation of The Hebrew OT). Eleven word group comparisons of Hebrew-Greek word equivalents involve a total of over 5200 Hebrew and Greek words . This study reveals that a search of the total number of the Greek (translation) word divided into the # of Hebrew(original) parallel word matching up with the Greek word in the grammatically corresponding place of each verse almost invariably yields a higher ratio (percentage) than the converse comparison – total Hebrew (original) divided into the matching & correlated Greek (translation) number. The words chosen here and in the Peshitta-Greek study are representative of the norm of such comparable pairs or groups that occur in sufficient numbers and correlate to each other with at least 20% correlation.

The Hebrew Primacy score ,dividing the 2656 Greek word total into 2303 matching Hebrew words, is 86.71%.
The LXX Primacy score , dividing the 2866 Hebrew word total into 1895 matching Greek words, is 66.12%
The words searched should be significantly related – 20% correlation or more.

Greek NT searches vs. aligned Syriac Peshitto : Syriac Peshitto searches vs. aligned Greek N.T.
Peshitta NT Primacy numbers vs. Westcott & Hort Greek NT Primacy numbers

Greek words Aramaic words	*Aramaic/Greek %*	# Aram	#Grk wds Grk/Ar %
(Gwynn's Critical edition of The Catholic Epistles & Revelation)			

W&H text compared to Peshitto in Apocalypse:	W&H text compared to Peshitto in Apocalypse:

("Earth","land")   **("Earth","land")**

γη – 91	91	88 **96.70%**	ארעא-88	88 80 90%
ארעא – 88				γη – 80
88/91= 96.7%				
80/88=91%				

("Great")   **("Great")**

μεγα-84	84	82 **97.62%**	רורבין , רבתא ,רבא – 77 89 83 93%
רמא-12			
רורבין , רבתא ,רבא =91 (77 match "mega")			
רמא-8 (5 match "mega")			Μεγα(λων)-83
82/84= **98** %			83/89 = **93.25** %

2 Peter- Revelation (including 1 Jn.)   **2 Peter- Revelation (including 1 Jn.)**
("From", "of", "out of")   **("From", "of", "out of")**

εκ, εξ -175			מן-364 (non-relative pronouns)
απο – 165			Εκ-196,απο-87- 283
340	340 283 **83.24%**		364 283 78%
283/418= 67.7%			
מן – 283			
283/340= 83.2%			

θεος-172(2 assoc. w/ Marya) 172	166 **96.51%**	אלהא-177	177 166 93.79%
אלהא-166			θεος-166
166/172 = 96.5%			
Total Greek Total Aramaic Avg. %		166/177= 93.79	
Total Aramaic		**Total Greek**	

687.000 619.000	**93.52%**	718.000 612 **88.93%**
Word Totals Aramaic Primacy Score: 89.84%		**Word Totals Greek Primacy Score:85.24%**

(6.)

Here is research of the Peshitto Aramaic Catholic Epistles and Revelation compared to The Westcott & Hort Greek edition of the same.

Four word group comparisons of Hebrew-Greek word equivalents involve a total of over 1300 Hebrew and Greek words . This study reveals that a search of the total number of the Greek (translation) word divided into the # of Hebrew(original) parallel word matching up with the Greek word in the grammatically corresponding place of each verse almost invariably yields a higher ratio (percentage) than the converse comparison – Total Hebrew (original)

divided into the matching Greek (translation) number.

Using the Hebrew OT-LXX model (see Pesh-Greek sheet) as a standard , the Peshitta-Greek N.T.results ,based on

over 1300 words, support the conclusion that The Greek Catholic Epistles and Revelation are translated from The Peshitta Aramaic text.

The Peshitta – Primary Score is 89.84% compared to The Greek Score of 85.24%.

Latin Vulgate searches vs. aligned Greek NT: Greek NT searches vs. aligned Latin Vulgate:	
Greek/Latin %	*Latin/Greek %*
<u>Greek NT Primacy numbers</u> <u>Latin Vulgate NT Primacy numbers</u>	
("Love") **("Love")**	
Carissim(i,o),caritas-43	Αγαπη,αγαπαω-293
Diligo,(ere)-4	Caritas, carissimi- 133
Αγαπαω, αγαπη-47	Diligo,diligit,etc.-96
Once αδελφος is translated carissimi	Dilect, dilex … 61
Contentione-1	
46/47=98% **98** Sorori-1	
Epulis-1	
Another N.T.search :	Fratres-1
carissimo,-(i)-3 294 -Did αγαπη come from 7 Latin words ? No, these 7 Latin roots came from 1 Greek root.	
diligit-78	**45**
6. diligit/αγαπη = 96/293 = 33%; (caritas,carissimi)/αγαπη = 133/293 or 45%	
αγαπω,αγαπη)-80	sum of above= 78%
80/81 = 99% **(99)**	Diligo,diligit total in N.T.search- 116 **78**
carissimo,-(i)-3	
diligit-119	
122	
αγαπω,αγαπη)-118	
118/122 = 97% **97**	**66.2**
Caritatum-93	Αγαπη,αγαπαω,ηγαπησεν,etc=320
7. (96+116)/320= 212/320=66.2%	
Αγαπη-93	Caritatum, Caritas=89

100%	**100**		89/320=27.8%	**27.8**
("World","Age")		**("World","Age")**		
Saeculam. Saeculum-106		Αιων, αιωνιος- 190		
Αιων, αιωνιος-97		Caelest(i,e,ubis)-3		
Aetern(a,am,ae,i,um,itatis)-86				
Greek/Latin=91%		Saeculor(a,am,ae,i,um,itatis)-87		
106+96(aetern*)=202		170/190=89%		
97+95=192				
192/202=95.0%	**95**			**89**
("Eternity", "Eternal")		**("Eternity", "Eternal", "Forever")**		
Aeternus- 94		Αιων, αιωνιος-196		
עלם-102		עלם- 213		
Αιων, αιωνιος-95		Saeculam, saeculum-95		
Aeternam, Aeternum-91				
Greek/Latin=100% **100**		Latin/Greek=186/196=94.9%	**94.9**	
Average % **98.17%**			**66.82%**	

(7.)

These data confirm The N.T. Vulgate is a translation of The Greek N.T.(Majority Text).This with The LXX-Hebrew O.T. is a control group.
The LXX is a translation of The Hebrew O.T.(Massoretic Text).

IV. The Theory:

The Majority Text Greek N.T. is a translation of The Peshitta N.T.
The Greek N.T.(Westcott & Hort) Catholic Epistles and Revelation are a translation of Peshitto text represented by the Critical Edition of Gwynn .

The tables above do not list all the verses of textual data , of course, as there are over 15,000 total references of verses in Aramaic, Greek, Hebrew & Latin analyzed and saved in files for this experiment.Of these 15,000 data, 6,000 are control data from The Latin Vulgate & Greek NT and The LXX & Hebrew OT.

There is no reason to believe more of the same type word studies will alter the general results and conclusions. The high volume of data establish these results as highly reliable.

Divine Contact-The Original New Testament Discovered

I conclude that the control data do support my initial hypothesis : The ratio of the number of <u>correlating original words</u> to <u>the total number of translation cognate word</u> in the text will exceed the ratio <u>of the number of correlated translated words</u> to <u>the total number of the original words</u>.

The other Peshitta & Greek data fit the control model of Semitic original vs. Greek translation . (The Latin Vulgate-Greek NT is also a control model, as we know the Latin is a translation of the Greek.)

Based on that confirmed hypothesis, the hypothesis receives standing as a theory until disproven.

I acknowledge that the ratio argument may be difficult to follow; the real test of the hypothesis is in the control results.The more of these I compile, the more confirmation I obtain. The word groups chosen must be equivalent and of sufficient number , generally > 100, to be valid. The correlation process must also be accurately done and totals must be accurate. If a root is searched, all forms of that root must be searched. Much of the search process is learned by practice. A novice will make many errors at first. Unrelated words and references must be weeded out of search results, or results will be skewed.

(8.)

Some will no doubt object that the words chosen were "cherry picked", results adverse to the hypothesis being discarded from the charts. That is not the case, though it may be charged against any experimenter who produces unusual or unpopular results. I have chosen the most obvious word relationships I could think of. They must be clearly related; I'm sure that poorly related word pairs may be found that would show different results. I am not interested in such poorly correlated words and such adverse results would not negate the hypothesis , since the words must first meet the requirement of 20% correlation , or actually be cognates (words entymologically related or close in meaning).

The data support the conclusion that **The Greek NT** (<u>The Byzantine Majority textform and Westcott & Hort's critical edition</u>) is a translation of The Peshitta text of The NT.

I welcome all challenges to this conclusion and encourage others to do more such studies or find other methods to determine which text is the original and which the translation.

Bibliography:

1.1905 Syriac Peshitta New Testament
    Published by British and Foreign Bible Society

2.1991 Byzantine/Majority Textform
    Keyed to Strongs and fully parsed.
Prepared by Maurice A. Robinson , Ph.D.
Department of Biblical Studies and Languages
Southeatern Baptist Theological Seminary
P.O. Box 1889

3. Online Hebrew Old Testament- Ver. 2.0
    Biblia Hebraica Stuttgartensia
Consonantal text Form
Copyright © 1967/77
Deutsche Bibelgesellschaft, Stuttgart

4. Greek Septuagint Version, 270 BC
    Edited by Alfred Rahlfs.
Text prepared and corrected by Dr. Maurice Robinson.
Verse synchronization by Stephen Long

5. Jerome's 405 A.D., Latin Vulgate. Public Domain.

6. 1881 Westcott-Hort Greek Text
with variant readings from the
UBS 3-4/Nestle 26-27 editions.
Prepared by Maurice A. Robinson, Ph.D.
Dept. of Biblical Studies and Languages
Southeastern Baptist Theological Seminary
P.O. Box 1889
Wake Forest, N. Carolina 27588

7. Online Bible Edition: Versions 1.22 -1.42
    Copyright © 1992-2004
    Copyright © 1995-2004, Online Bible Foundation
    12 Birkfield Place, Carluke, Lanarkshire, Scotland, Ml8
    Copyright © 1987-2004, Timnathserah Inc.
    11 Holmwood St., Winterbourne, Ontario, Canada. N0B
    Free updates : http://www.OnlineBible.Net

8. Microsoft Word 2002 (10.2627.2625)
    Copyright © Microsoft Corporation 1983-2001. All rights reserved.

(I have used CodeFinder 1.21 – 1.23 Bible Codes software , Microsoft Excel 2002 , and Randy Ingermanson's CodeCracker 1.0 beta for this experiment.)

So what is a Z Score or a Chi Squared or log of probability ? They are all statistics describing the probability of an event occurring.
A Z Score of 1.0 represents approx. a 1 in 4 chance; 2.0 represents a 5 in 100 chance; 3.0 a 4 in 1000 chance, etc.
As it grows, a Z score's significance grows exponentially; for instance, 5.0 represents a probability of about 1 in a million; 6.0 – about 6 in a billion.
7.0 has a probability of 9 in a trillion ! Some of the Z Scores in this experiment for one Name are greater than 20; some in my original experiment
are greater than 100. A Z Score of 20 has a probability of 3 in 10 to the 88th power! 21.0 has 1 in 10 to the 97th power !

Divine Contact-The Original New Testament Discovered

A Z Score of 100 represents approx. a 1 in 10 to the 2,171[st] power !
The probability formula is:$(1/SQRT(2*PI))*2.718^{-(|Z^2|/2)}$.

One of the marks of validity in a scientific theory is its power to predict results in certain applications of its premises. I would like to list some predictions based on my hypothesis stated above .

I. The Peshitta Aramaic NT will be shown by solid textual, linguistic, grammatical,historical and logical evidence to be the basis for The Greek NT.

II. The Greek NT , conversely, will prove to be a translation of the above, not the original NT language and text

New Testament Entropy

I will make this simple: I have a program called Codecracker, written by Randy Ingermanson, author of , Who Wrote The Bible Code ?
This software is designed to search for codes in a text, either Hebrew,Greek or English. It also analyzes the text and gives statistics, such as
the total number of words and number of vocabulary words. The latter two functions are all I was concerned with in this study. My hypothesis
is that a translation of an extensive text will simplify that text by using one translation word, more often than not, for two or more
original words, thus reducing the vocabulary to total word number ratio.
A simple example for Greek to English translation is "Agapay" and "Philay" – two Greek words translated "Love" in English.
Here are three versions of The Gospel of Luke:
The KJV is a translation of the Byzantine Greek text: Its Vocab. to Total Words ratio is 9.2%
The Byzantine Greek has 23.2% ratio- much higher than the English version.
The Western (Gwilliams & Pusey) Peshitta Luke has a 29.6% ratio- significantly higher than The Greek version.

Luke KJV

Tot.Words	25939
Distinct Wds.	2387
Dist/Tot.%	9.20%

Luke Byz Greek

Tot.Words	19887
Distinct Wds.	4608
Dist/Tot.%	23.17%

Divine Contact-The Original New Testament Discovered

Luqa Peshitta

Tot.Words	15235
Distinct Wds.	4502
Dist/Tot.%	29.55%

Following is a comparison of the Gospels and Acts , along with comparisons of the entire NT texts for the aforementioned versions as well as Westcott & Hort's Greek NT, The Old Syriac of John, The Eastern Peshitta NT ,The Hebrew and LXX Torahs and the KJV Torah.

My purpose is to show that an original text will have a higher ratio of distinct words to total words

than a translation of the same original text. If this is so, and it seems to hold true here (See also Hebrew Torah versus KJV Torah), then

the Greek text is a translation of The Peshitta as the KJV NT is a translation of the Greek NT.

	Luke KJV	KJV/Gk	Mat. KJV	KJV/Gk	John KJV	Acts KJV	Mark KJV	KJV/Gk	KJV NT	Weymouth NT	
Tot.Words	25939	1.3043	23211	1.238			15166	1.30	184117	1.31	
Distinct Wds.	2387		2062				1675	Avg. KJV.	8526		
Dist/Tot.	9.20%		8.88%				11.04%		9.58%	4.63%	
Tot. Trigrams			94543						739165	802792	
Distinct Trigrams			4287						5978	6283	
Dist/Tot.			4.53%				4.53%		0.809%	0.783%	

	Luke Byz Greek	-Gk/Pesh	Mat Grk.	Gk/Pesh	John Grk.	Gk/Pesh	Acts Grk.	Gk/Pesh	Mark Grk	Gk/Pesh	Byz. NT	Gk/Pesh	T.R. NT
Tot.Words	19887	1.3053	18745	1.34065	15919	1.28286	18680	1.21	11671	1.33	140258	1.28	140720
Distinct Wds.	4608	Gk./KJV	3957	Gk./KJV	2586		4580		2899	Avg. Byz. Gk./KJV	17184	Gk./KJV	17266
Dist/Tot.	23.17%	2.52	21.11%	2.38	16.24%		24.52%		24.84%	22.18%	2.31	12.25%	2.65	12.27%
Tot. Trigrams	86592		91877		72474		96835		96835		690960		693237
Distinct Trigrams	3906		3948		3479		3964		3964		5509		5509
Dist/Tot.	4.51%		4.30%	0.95	4.80%		4.09%		4.09%	4.36%	0.96	0.80%	0.99	0.79%

	Luqa Peshitta		Matti Peshitta		John Peshitta	Acts Peshitta		Marqus Peshitta		Peshitta NT		East Pesh NT
Tot.Words	15235		13982		12409	15384		8796		109651		101324
Distinct Wds.	4502	Pesh/Gk.	4069	Pesh/Gk.	2753	Pesh/Gk.	4338	Pesh/Gk	2871	Avg. Pesh.	Pesh/Gk	16439	Tot. Pesh.	15244
Dist/Tot.	29.55%	1.28	29.10%	1.38	22.19%	1.37	28.20%	1.15	32.64%	28.54%	1.29	14.99%	1.22	15.04%
Tot. Trigrams	62591		57794		48503	65811		36331		461041		424233
Distinct Trigrams	5245		5028		4219	5042		4338		7395		7313
Dist/Tot.	8.38%		8.70%		8.70%	7.66%		11.94%	9.08%	1.604%	2.01	1.724%	

	John Old Syriac	W&H Greek NT	UBS Grk. NT
Tot.Words	14201	137680	157501
Distinct Wds.	2777	17292	19635
Dist/Tot.	19.55%	12.56%	12.47%
Tot. Trigrams	55664	679751	
Distinct Trigrams	4109	5517	
Dist/Tot.	7.38%	0.812%	

	James Peshitta	1 John Peshitta	
Tot.Words	9851	8091	
Distinct Wds.	1444	1547.00	Avg.
Dist/Tot.	14.66%	19.12%	16.15%
Tot. Trigrams			
Distinct Trigrams			

Divine Contact-The Original New Testament Discovered

Dist/Tot.

The Torah is a good model by which to test the above hypothesis of Vocab. To Total Words ratios. The LXX Torah is a known translation of The Hebrew Torah, made about 270 B.C. in Alexandria , Egypt under the order of the Greek King Ptolemy.

	Torah- Koren Hebrew	Torah LXX		Torah- KJV		LXXE				
Tot.Words	79976	124519	**1.55695**	156739	**1.95983**	157879	**1.27**			
Distinct Wds.	12830			11499		4796		Heb/KJV		Heb/LXX
Dist/Tot.	**16.04%**	**9.23%**	**1.74**	**3.06%**				**5.24**		**1.74**
Tot. Trigrams	304803			526064		633173				
Distinct Trigrams	7449			5330		5801				
Dist/Tot.	2.44%	1.01%		0.92%						

Theoretically, a translation should exhibit less variety and a smaller vocabulary/# words ratio, simply because a translator's goal is to simplify a text to make it readable for his audience, hence, in more cases than not, he will translate two or more original words with one translation vocab. word.Often he will also simply drop original words that seem superfluous to the translation language syntax,grammar and style.

Notice that the Vocab./# Words ratio for the Hebrew Torah is 16% , the LXX has 9.2% and The KJV Torah has 3 %.
Notice that the Vocab./# Words ratio for <u>the Peshitta NT</u> is 15% , <u>the Greek NT</u> has 12.3% and The KJV NT has 4.6 %.

Divine Contact-The Original New Testament Discovered

This ratio trend holds for all comparisons in the Gospels and Acts; The Vocab./Total # wds. ratio is smaller for the translation of a text than for its original.

Some other notable facts are : The Old Syriac of John's Gospel has a Vocab. to Total Words ratio of 19.55% - lower than the Peshitta Gospel of John's 22.19% but higher than The Byzantine Greek John's 16.24%.
This suggests that the Old Syriac not a translation of the Greek but a revision of The Peshitta toward a Greek exemplar.

The Eastern Peshitta shows also a slightly higher <u>Vocab. to Total Words</u> ratio than the Western Peshitta- only 0.05 percentage points higher, but enough to suggest that the few textual differences in The Eastern version may be original and the Western readings in error.
This is not conclusive, since the difference is so small and the Eastern text used here is an imperfect collation of the Western text corrected by hand to conform to Eastern readings in notable places and also without the five Western books in the General Epistles and Revelation.
On the other hand, the fact that the Western canon results are so close to the Eastern canon results strongly supports the Western canon in Aramaic to be the original behind the Byzantine Greek and Critical Greek NT.

Daniel 2:4-7:28 in Aramaic has 3603 words;The LXX of that passage has 5388 words.

The entire book of Daniel in Hebrew-Aramaic has 5949 words and 2488 distinct words. That is a 41.82% ratio for the Aramaic-Hebrew Daniel.
The book of Daniel in The LXX has 9932 words and 2431 distinct words.
24.48% of the words in Greek Daniel are distinct- very close to the 24.84% for Greek Mark, the smallest NT book studied.
Mark has 11,671 words, the closest total to this of Daniel. Smaller books will tend to have higher ratios of distinct words, all else being equal.

The Gospel of Mark ratio and the average for all the Gospels is about the same as that for The Greek of Daniel . The Peshitta Gospels and The Hebrew-Aramaic Daniel have significantly higher ratios than their Greek counterparts.
I predicted, before running Codecracker on The LXX of Daniel, that on the basis of the Greek book of Mark statistics, the LXX of Daniel would have 9262 words and 2311 distinct words. The word total was based on the Torah ratio of Greek LXX words to Hebrew words and the total number of Hebrew-Aramaic words in Daniel. 1.556900319 is the first ratio; 5949 is the total for Hebrew-Aramaic Daniel.

My estimates were off by 7% and 5% , respectively.
9262 is 93% of 9932 and 2311 is 95% of 2488.

What does all this mean ?
It means that <u>***The Greek NT***</u> ***looks like a translation of The Aramaic Peshitta NT. The stats for*** <u>***the Greek NT***</u> ***can be used to predict the results for the Greek OT (LXX) , which we know is translated from The Hebrew-Aramaic OT.***

I don't know how many more ways this can be demonstrated. I have enlisted Bible codes, Alep-Tau codes, word pair comparisons, letter frequency analysis, historical evidence, grammatical evidence and doctrinal – inspirational evidence, as well as numerical structure - (though not formally). Added to the split word examples, word plays, poetic nature of The Peshitta , and plain common sense position of Peshitta primacy extensively researched and written by others (notably Paul Younan and associates of Peshitta.org), there is also the "*Lost in Translation*" study, involving the loss of prepositions, pronouns and conjunctions in **the Greek NT** and in

the LXX Greek OT, compared to the greater numbers of the same in **The Peshitta NT** and Hebrew OT.
The same phenomenon can be observed with the numbers of Divine Names in the Greek and Aramaic texts of the NT.
Many thousands of data have been compiled , all supporting Peshitta primacy.

If there are more proofs, they will be found; the evidence will mount skyward, pouring down earthward from Heaven, till it "cover the earth as the waters cover the sea", and then perhaps, just perhaps, brutish men will acknowledge God in Heaven , and that He has spoken to mankind and left the record of it in the Aramaic of The Peshitta and The Hebrew of Moses and the Prophets.

Of course it will be so, as it is written:
For my thoughts are not your thoughts, neither are your ways my ways, saith the LORD.
For as the heavens are higher than the earth, so are my ways higher than your ways, and my thoughts than your thoughts.
For as the rain cometh down, and the snow from heaven, and returneth not thither, but watereth the earth, and maketh it bring forth and bud, that it may give seed to the sower, and bread to the eater:
So shall my word be that goeth forth out of my mouth: it shall not return unto me void, but it shall accomplish that which I please, and it shall prosper in the thing whereto I sent it. –Isaiah 55:8-11

Isa 11:9 They shall not hurt nor destroy in all my holy mountain: for the earth shall be full of the knowledge of the LORD, as the waters cover the sea.

Aftermath: **I recently came upon the following on the internet from a German study-**
Multi-layer analysis of translation corpora: methodological issues and practical implications.

Silvia Hansen
Department of Applied Linguistics,
Translation and Interpreting
Universit"at des Saarlandes
66041 Saarbr"ucken, Germany
S.Hansen@mx.uni-saarland.de
Elke Teich
Department of Applied Linguistics,
Translation and Interpreting
Universit"at des Saarlandes
44041 Saarbr"ucken, Germany
&
Department of Linguistics
University of Sydney, Australia
E.Teich@mx.uni-saarland.de

1 Introduction
The present paper discusses an analysis scenario in which instances of features of various linguistic

Lexical density
For determining lexical density, we use the WordList function of the Word-

levels need to be extracted in more than one language. The concrete application discussed is one from translation studies. Our main theoretical goal is the empirical testing of hypotheses about the specific properties of translations (see below). As a secondary goal, we want to elaborate the specific requirements on tools and techniques for a corpus-based analysis of translations and ultimately build up a translation corpus workbench that caters for the specific informational needs of researchers, teachers and students in translation studies. While there is a lot of experience in the construction of monolingual corpus resources (tree banks; e.g., (Marcus et al, 1993) for English, or (Brants, 1999; Plaehn, 2000; K¨onig and Lezius, 2000) for German), linguistically-annotated multilingual corpora remain rare, and translation corpora even rarer (with the exception of corpora for statistical machine translation and translation memories (example-based translation), but these are typically "raw" or only shallow-annotated). It is commonly assumed in translation studies that translations are specific kinds of texts that are not only different from their original source language (SL) texts, but also from comparable original texts in the same language as the target language (TL). For instance, it has often been observed that translations tend to be longer than their SL originals, on the one hand, and that they are simpler than their SL originals or than comparable original texts in the TL, on the other hand.

2.1 Formulation of hypotheses

Simplification. Simplification means that translations tend to use simpler language than comparable original texts (cf. Section 1). Taking lexical density as a possible measure providing evidence for simplification, the following more con-

First, additional hypotheses about the specific nature of translations relating to the source language can be formulated. One such hypothesis is the following:
* In translations, the source language tends to shine through.

<u>Normalization/Shining-through.</u> *One of the_____ register features of the register of scientific writing in English that also holds for popularized scientific*

Smith Tools, which matches a function word list (here: for English and German) with the words in a corpus. On this basis, lexical density can be calculated. The results for lexical density for the register of political speeches for all of the English originals, the German translations and the German comparable texts are shown in Figure 2. According to (H1), the lexical density in translations should be lower than in a monolingually comparable corpus. The analysis shows that in fact, lexical density is lower in the German translations, if only slightly, and we can thus interpret this result as simplification. In addition, this result may be interpreted as normalization and count as counter evidence to shining-through.

Simplification.

Translations tend to use simpler language than original texts in the same language as the TL, possibly to optimize the readability of the target language text. Possible measures for simplification are average sentence length, <u>lexical density</u> and type-token ratio, the latter being a standard measure for the vocabulary variation in a text.

Explicitation. Translations tend to be more explicit *than comparable original texts in the same language as the TL. For instance, they may use more optional elements (cf. (Baker, 1996, 180)), such as daß/that as complementizer, or employ more explicit (less densely packed) linguistic renderings of a given semantic content vs. less explicit*

ones (more densely packed), e.g., more conjunctions vs. prepositions. Conjunctions indicate that logico-semantic relations, such as temporal or causal ones, are made explicit, prepositions indicate a less explicit lexico-grammatical rendering of such relations (cf. (Halliday and Matthiessen, 1999)). See examples (1) and (2) for illustration.2
(1) After she had arrived at the airport, she caught a bus to Central Station.
(2) After arrival at the airport she caught a

texts is the extensive use of passive. In German, passive is a typical feature of scientific texts as well, but there is also a wide range of other constructions which fulfil a similar function (i.e., not specifying or underspecifyng the Agent of a process). These constructions occur frequently in German original texts of the given register, e.g., constructions with lassen (let) plus a reflexive verb, impersonal constructions with man

bus to Central Station.

2.2 Techniques of analysis and analysis results
The empirical testing of each of the hypotheses formulated above places different requirements on the corpus analysis techniques to be used.

(EO is English Original, G-T is German Translation, G-O is German Original)

E-O G-T G-O
(one) or sein zu (be to) constructions; henceforth these will be called passive alternatives. For some examples see (3)-(5) below.3

Lexical Density 50.62 48.67 49.55
Figure 2: Lexical density in E-O, G-T and G-O political speeches)
While calculating lexical density and carrying out string searches are standard functions of a concordance tool, such as WordSmith (Scott, 1996), operate on raw texts, for the others, various kinds of annotation are needed to extract the desired information, and these annotations can only partly carried out automatically.

Lexical density. For determining lexical density, we use the WordList function of the Word-Smith Tools, which matches a function word list here: for English and German) with the words corpus. On this basis, lexical density can be calculated. The results for lexical density for the register of political speeches for all of the English originals, the German translations and the German comparable texts are shown in Figure 2. According to (H1), the lexical density in translations should be lower than in a monolingually comparable corpus. The analysis shows that in fact, lexical density is lower in the German translations, if only slightly, and we can thus interpret this result as simplification. In addition, this result may be interpreted as normalization and count as counter evidence to shining-through.

Other scholarly studies like this exist and define and use Lexical Density measurements to determine originals and translations.

Suffice it to say that _Lexical Density_ is essentially the ratio of vocab. words to Total words. That ratio will be lower in a translation than in its original. This among other facts is confirmed here. I can find no evidence that anyone else beside myself has applied this method to testing _The Greek NT_ &

__The Peshitta NT__ to determine which is the original.

Chapter 16 -<u>Lost in Translation</u>

I have observed that <u>The Aramaic Peshitta New Testament</u> contains many more personal pronouns and prepositions (thousands more,in fact) than <u>The Greek New Testament</u>. I believe this can be shown as evidence to support the primacy (originality) of The Peshitta , and evidence that <u>The Greek NT</u> is a translation of <u>The Peshitta NT</u>.

This is a comparison of two versions of the NT- **The Peshitta NT** and **The Byzantine Greek NT**. This study is based on an experiment , using two English translations of the above versions: <u>James Murdock's 1846 translation of The Peshitta</u> and <u>The King James Version of the NT</u> , also known as <u>The Authorized Version</u>. The basic premise and hypothesis to be proved in this experiment is fairly simple: It is universally acknowledged that these two versions , **The Peshitta NT** in Aramaic and **The Greek NT** (all text types) are related in that one of them is an ancient translation of the other. Generally, according to most textual scholars, the Peshitta is supposed to be translated from **The Greek NT** circa A.D. 400.The alternative view is , of course , that The Greek texts are a translation, or translations of The Peshitta. This is the view of scholars of The Church of The East for time immemorial. I propose that **The Peshitta NT** is the original behind **The Greek NT** and that this fact may be demonstrated by computer analysis of the prepositions, pronouns and conjunctions of each version. A famous proponent of the Peshitta primacy view was George Gwilliam , who published and co authored **Tetraevangelium Sanctum** with Phillip Edward Pusey , in 1901. This was the first scholarly collation of **The Peshitta NT** mss. in an edition of The Gospels, to be followed by another of The Pauline Epistles. His partner had died before the editions were published, but I think it is safe to assume that he shared the same position with regard to The Peshitta. This was an unpopular position in the world of academia. The prevailing trend was that Rabbula, a Syrian bishop from AD 410-450 , had created The Peshitta from Greek mss. and "The Old Syriac" version. The Old Syriac was embodied in only two mss., both incomplete versions of the Gospels, dated from the 4th and 5th centuries. One of these manuscripts (Sinaiticus Syriacus, 4th cent.) is a palimpsest (ms. that has been reused by erasing an original work written on leather and written over the old text.) There are many missing sections in the text, and many differences in readings from the Curetonian (The 5th century ms.).

There is no manuscript or historical support for Old Syriac in any other NT books (Acts through Revelation). Though some have hypothesized the existence of the same, no one has produced anything. It is strange that there is no coherent support for this text *__in any NT book__* (the two mss. disagree as often as not in their variations from The Peshitta text).

__Regardless the view one holds about The Peshitta or Old Syriac, most scholars seem to agree that all Aramaic versions are translations of a Greek original. Most seem to believe in an original Greek NT. I have researched and written on this subject considerably for the past five years and have been a student of Greek and NT Textual Criticism for the past thirty years , and I believe there is a simple test to determine which version is the translation and which the original, when confronted with two texts, one of which is the translation of the other.__

Divine Contact-The Original New Testament Discovered

Simply put, the one with the most words wins. Specifically and more precisely, the translator(s) will tend to lose some of the information of the original in the process of extensive translation work. There is always something "<u>lost in translation</u>". This can be examined by comparing cognate words (in a loose sense,words in two or more languages with the same essential meaning) , making sure that we examine simple, straightforward related word pairs , one Greek, one Aramaic, counting the number of each in the selected text, whether Matthew , Mark , or the entire NT.

For example, "υδωρ–**hudor**",(Greek word for "water") occurs 570 times in **The LXX** – The ancient 3rd cent. BC Greek Septuagint translation of the **Hebrew OT**. The Hebrew cognate ("Mayim"-water) occurs 582 times . That means the Greek translators dropped the word 12 times in the process of translation. **The LXX** has the word for "**Spirit**" ("Πνευμα –**Pneuma**") 307 times ; The **Hebrew OT** has the word for "**Spirit**" ("**Ruach**") 392 times. The translators dropped the word or used another word for it 85 times. This is the rule for relationship between a translation and its original.
The discrepancies are amplified when less significant words are examined , like prepositions , conjunctions and personal pronouns.

Let me illustrate, again with <u>the LXX</u> and <u>Hebrew OT</u>:

(These statistics are taken from English translations of each version, as most would be almost impossible to ascertain from the original Hebrew or Greek. The only one I could verify in Hebrew is "And".)

Old Testament Comparisons of Conjunctions,Prepositions & Pronouns in Hebrew & LXX Bibles

English word Greek word Hebrew word	Versions	# Words LXXE	# Words Hebrew	Heb. to Greek Ratio Heb/LXX %
"His" Greek αυτου; Heb. ו-	LXXE-Young's Lit. Trans.	**6685**	**6917**	**103.47%**
"Me" Greek με,εμε; Heb. אתי,לי-י-ני	LXXE-Young's Lit. Trans.	**2445**	**1546**	63.23%
"My" Greek μου,εμου; Heb. י-	LXXE-Young's Lit. Trans.	**3833**	**4006**	**104.51%**
"Us" Greek ημιν,ημας; Heb. נו-	LXXE-Young's Lit. Trans.	**746**	**675**	90.48%
"Them","Their"Greek αυτων,-ους,-οις; Heb.אתם-,ם-,הם-LXXE-Young's Lit. Trans.(# vrses)	**5214**	**4543**	87.13%
"Our" Greek ημων; Heb. נו-	LXXE-Young's Lit. Trans.	**865**	**795**	91.91%
"Of" (not calculated in stats as most are Genitive constructs, not preps.) LXXE-Young's Lit. Trans.		(not calculated in stats.)		
"In" Greek εν or dative; Heb. ב–	LXXE-Young's Lit. Trans.	10020	**11239**	**112.17%**
"By" Greek δια, εν, υπο or dative; Heb. ב–	LXXE-Young's Lit. Trans.	1815	**2163**	**119.17%**
"With" Greek παρα,προς, εν, or dative; Heb. ב– , עם LXXE-Young's Lit. Trans.	4435	**4166**	93.93%
"In,By,With"-combined Greek εν or dative,etc.;Heb.(ב–),etc. LXXE-Young's Lit. Trans.	16270	17568	107.98%
"From" **Greek** απο, εκ, w-gen.; **Heb.** מן , מ-	LXXE-Young's Lit. Trans.	3308	**4059**	**122.70%**
"To" Greek προς,επι,εις ; Heb. אל,את,ל–	LXXE-Young's Lit. Trans.	17256	14859	86.11%
"Unto" Greek εις,προς,επι ; Heb. את,אל,ל–	LXXE-Young's Lit. Trans.	37	5539	**14970.27%**
"Into" Greek εις,προς, Heb. אל,ב-,ל–	LXXE-Young's Lit. Trans.	1466	803	**54.77%**
"To,Unto,Into" *combined*	LXXE-Young's Lit. Trans.	**18759**	**21201**	**113.02%**
"And" Greek και, ("kai") Heb. ו–	LXX - Hebrew.	45158	**51027**	**112.60%**
"But" Greek δε , Heb. ו–	LXX-Young's Lit. Trans.	**3153**		
"And","But" Combined –Greek και,δε,αλλα Heb. ו–	LXX - Hebrew.	48305	51027	105.63%
Total Preps. & Conjunctions, Possessive Pronouns-		97160	104778	107.84%

*A study of **The LXX** & Hebrew of the Prophets shows that there are 4.5% more Και's than matching waw conjunctions.*
and 11% more δε's than matching waw conjunctions I have adjusted the totals for these conjunctions accordingly."Kai" and "de" may be descriminately.

added routinely to make for smoother Greek out of a Semitic original

In six out of the four grey & two yellow shaded sections (color version), the Hebrew text translation has more words than the Septuagint in English .These grey groups are based on a particular Hebrew preposition or conjunction.

"To,Unto,Into" in blue, above, are most likely translated from The Hebrew prep. "Lamed", and should be grouped together as one number:

18759   21201   113.02%

*The total for "To,Unto,Into" in Hebrew is **113.02** % of **the LXX** number (18759) . That is also close to the overall result of **107.66 %** (Hebrew divided by LXX). I managed to obtain a real-time Hebrew count (**50960**) for the waw consecutive (Young's Literal Translation is so literal that it translates almost everyone of these as "and" – **46409** times) and the actual Greek total for "kai" (**47451**) .*
"But" in English is usually translated from the Hebrew waw consecutive like "And"is; It should be grouped with "And".
"In,By,With" are combined because they frequently reflect a common Hebrew preposition (–כ).

The numbers for conjunctions in The Torah are: Hebrew (BHS) waw consec. = 13785
LXX kai = 11704; de = 1546; Total = 13250. Hebrew/LXX = 13785/13250, or 104%.
That is very close to the adjusted conjunction total for the Heb. OT/LXX of 105%.
The Torah LXX is the most accurate part of the LXX and in closest agreement with The Hebrew.
Most of The Hebrew prepositions and conjunctions are one or two letters , are very common, and therefore easily dropped or missed in translations.Often they are considered redundant in non Semitic languages and are therefore often taken for granted (in my humble opinion).That is why there are such discrepancies in the numbers in Young's (a very literal translation) and The LXX English. The totals above exclude most pronouns, as they are usually more than one letter or attached to a separated prep. making them more obvious and less susceptible to omission.
The blue shaded section marks prepositions; the red marks the conjunctions; Yellow marks one letter Hebrew pronouns.
Now let's look at The NT numbers from The Peshitta and The Byzantine Greek, represented in Murdock's English translation and The King James Version, respectively:

New Testament Comparisons of Conjunctions,Prepositions & Pronouns in Aramaic & Greek NT's

	Murdock	YLT	Peshitta/Greek %
In	3206	3289	97.48%
By	1072	590	181.69%
To	5887	6575	89.54%
For	2576	1758	146.53%
Into	384	288	133.33%
Unto	118	571	20.67%
From	1215	878	138.38%

With	1459	1216	119.98%
On	806	600	134.33%
Upon	312	415	75.18%
Total reps.	17035	16180	105.28%
And	12713	9324	136.35% *(From Aramaic & Greek)*
But	1830	2856	64.08% *(From Aramaic & Greek)*
"And"+"But"	14543	12180	119.40% *(From Aramaic & Greek)*
Me	577	664	86.90%
My	891	622	143.25%
"Me"+"My"	1468	1286	114.15%
Us	412	330	124.85%
Our	646	328	196.95%
"Us"+"Our"	1058	658	160.79%
Him	1641	2001	82.01%
His	1634	1276	128.06%
	37379	33581	111.31%

"**And**" is from Aram. (-ו), דין, & Grk.και;
"**But**"is from Aram.דין,(-ו), אלא, & Grk. Αλλα, & δε

"And" is based on real-time Aramaic and Greek word counts, not the English translations.
The W&H text has about 8995 kai's (96% of TR); Byzantine has 9266 (99% of TR).
*Eleven of the seventeen words occur in greater numbers in The Aramaic representation (Murdock) than in The Greek rep. (**Young's Literal Translation**). **Ten out of fifteen** of the grouped sections representing **The Peshitta NT** show more words than in **The Greek NT**.*
"To" & "For" usually are translated in the English from the Aramaic preposition and proclitic "Lamed"; they should be grouped together.
The personal pronouns "Me" & "My" are identical in Aramaic and attached to the end of some other word; they should also be grouped together; The same applies to "Us" & "Our".

Most of The Aramaic prepositions and conjunctions are one letter attached to the beginning of another word, are very common, and are therefore easily dropped or missed in translations. That is why there are such discrepancies in the numbers in Murdock (a literal translation) and The KJV (a literal translation of The TR Greek NT).

Color coding was used for the color edition:
Blue shaded sections cover prepositions; purple is for conjunctions; tan is for possessive pronouns.
The key index word for both comparisons is "And"; It is the "Waw" in both Hebrew & Aramaic, and it occurs far more often than translated in both languages. It occurs over 51,000 times in The Hebrew Bible, while the Greek equivalent "kai" occurs only 47,451 times (93% as often). Now we know that The LXX is a translation of the Hebrew, so the translators dropped 7% of the original "waws" in the process.

Divine Contact-The Original New Testament Discovered

If we were asked to believe The Hebrew were a translation of The LXX, we would be required to believe the Hebrew translator(s) added 3,500 conjunctive "Waws" to the translation (a 7% addition to the original, consistently throughout the whole OT !)
Which would be easier to believe, 7% of the conjuctions dropped or 3,500 "Waws" (7%) created and added to the original throughout?

The situation is very similar for The NT comparison: The Peshitta has 12713 "Waw" ("And") proclitics; The Textus Receptus Greek NT has 9324 of "kai"("and") . Did Zorba The Greek drop 3389 (27%) (12713-9268 = 3389; 3389/12713 = 27%) of the Aramaic Waw's in his Greek translation or did an Aramaean translator invent and add 3389 (36%) (3389/9324 = 36%) more And's to a translation from Greek into Aramaic ?
Considering The LXX as a model example, I think the answer is plain.

The overall averages are for the two sets of comparisons.
Waws omitted : 7% for The Greek LXX; 27% for The TR Greek N.T. !
The ratio of these waw conjunctions to the whole text (letter numbers) is: Hebrew OT- 4.25%; Aramaic NT-2.75%. The ratio for The LXX is 6.15% . The ratio of The (TR & Byzantine) NT Greek "kai" to the whole text (letter numbers) is 4.03%. ! (Westcott &Hort has 3.96%.) The ratio of the Hebrew 4.2 to the LXX 6.1 is 0.69.1, or 69%; The ratio of the Aramaic Peshitta's 2.75%. to The Greek NT's 4.0% is 0.687, or 69% ! That means the statistical relationship of the Greek NT to the Peshitta in its number of the conjunction varies almost identically as the LXX compares to The Hebrew Bible (Both are 69% ratios) ! (Westcott & Hort in the comparison yields 70.7%.)

(Please pause here for prayer & meditation.)

The data for both studies is significant; we have studied 104,778 words from the Hebrew Bible. There are 1,196,925 letters in the Hebrew Bible.Even if we conservatively assign only one letter to each Hebrew word (some are 2 or 3 letters), this means we have examined 8.7% of the data of the entire Hebrew Bible ! Doing the same for the NT study, these 37,379 Aramaic words would constitute at least 8.1% of the Peshitta NT ! That is a lot of data !
Most statistical analysis requires only roughly one millionth of the total data population to obtain reliable statistics.
Did the Hebrew Bible result from Hebrew translators dreaming up and adding thousands of words to The Greek LXX ? We know better;The LXX is not the original, The Hebrew text is !
The LXX is the result of a Greek translator dropping thousands of words from the original Hebrew text (6000+ preps,conj. & pronouns in this study alone !)
How about The Peshitta ? Did Aramaeans add thousands of words to an original Greek text in translating The Peshitta ? I have detected 3700+ words more in The Peshitta than in the Greek text, through the above analysis.
The Hebrew OT and The Peshitta NT have 7 % to 11% more of these conjunctions, prepositions & pronouns than the Greek versions. We know the LXX was translated from The Hebrew text. May we not safely conclude that the Greek NT is also a translation, according to

the same model as _The LXX_ – Hebrew Bible relationship ?Someone either added 11% (3798 occurrences of these 18 Aramaic words) of Greek words when translating to Aramaic , or someone else omitted 10% of the Aramaic occurrences (3798) in a translation into Greek.

The results of this study confirm all the other studies I have done and presented thus far:
*The Peshitta is not a translation from **the Greek NT**; The Greek is a translation from the Peshitta in the same way **The LXX** is a translation of <u>The Hebrew Bible</u>.*

Note: These statistics have been the result of several recounts and very close scrutiny by one who has studied Greek for 30 years, Hebrew on and off for 25 years & Aramaic for perhaps 5 years. Some of the searches showed inaccurate results initially in MS Word searches, due to presence of commas and quotation marks in some translations as well as grammatical and orthographical reasons ("Kai" is sometimes compounded with "Ekeinos" & "Ekei to form "Kakeinos" & "Kakei", as well as with the Greek particle "αν" to form "Καν".
Someone not familiar with Greek grammar would likely miss these occurrences and miscalculate the totals.Even <u>Strong's Concordance</u> total for "Kai" does not count the compound form. I may have missed some as well, though I have spent probably 80 hours on this project counting and recalculating the stats on a fairly fast computer with lots of RAM.

Re 7:10 וקעין בקלא רבא ואמרין פורקנא לאלהן ולדיתב על כורסיא ולאמרא

And they cried with a loud voice, saying, Salvation to our God and to Him who sits upon the throne, and unto the Lamb.

Summary- Chapter 17

All the data compiled using Codefinder & Codecracker , Online Bible, MS Word, Text Stat, MS Excel for the above analyses of The Peshitta New Testament and The Greek New Testament , Hebrew OT and LXX Greek OT easily amount to more than 27 million data points . The Divine Names experiment alone analyzes a total of 27 million ELS's in The Peshitta.The data affirm as a body the hypothesis I posited and tested in the Divine Names experiment:

If anyone objects to my results in the long codes I have found, there is my Divine Names experiment with Codefinder and my results of searches in the NT with CodeCracker software, both of which give very similar statistics that validate the hypothesis that codes exist in The Peshitta New Testament, which follows here:

" If God were to put codes in the Bible, he would leave a signature in it using the names and titles of God which are mentioned in the plain Bible text, and insure that they occur in highly significant numbers, far beyond or below statistically expected numbers. These would constitute a divine signature of the author of the books individually, the separate Testaments and the Bible as a whole."

Most of this book is concerning The New Testament in Aramaic, not The Hebrew Old Testament, though I have included results for The Hebrew Torah. I have tested other Hebrew Old Testament books as well, with results very similar to The Torah and The Peshitta NT. None of the analysis results discussed in this book or of those unmentioned analyses that I have performed provides dissenting evidence from the aforesaid hypothesis.

I therefore and hereby conclude, on the basis of the volume of the data accumulated and the exhaustive nature of the searches in Codefinder, Codecracker, Online Bible and MS Word ,MS Excel and Text Stat, that the scientific , mathematical and linguistic data powerfully support the following conclusions :

1. *The God and Christ of God of <u>The New Testament</u> exist and are exactly Who and What that New Testament says they are.*

2. *<u>The God Whose Names are recorded in The Hebrew and Aramaic Testaments did put codes into The Bible</u> , particularly <u>The Aramaic Peshitta New Testament,</u> as embodied in The Critical edition included in Codefinder, and essentially the same as the Online Bible version of The Peshitta NT, with the 27 book canon and in The Eastern book order.*

3. *<u>That same God is The Author of The New Testament.</u>*

4. *The evidence ,including the word studies presented,also conclusively supports the position that <u>The Greek New Testament was translated from The same Aramaic Peshitta</u> text , or one very similar to it .*

5. *The New Testament in which these scientific proofs exist is absolutely true in all its statements, i.e.- infallible- historically, theologically, prophetically, scientifically, grammatically, geographically and textually-where it presents data concerning what pertains to the claimed statements and activities of God, Christ and The Holy Spirit. Whatever statements or actions are attributed to humans , angels or demons are also accurately recorded and are true history, though , unlike Divine statements, may not be necessarily true statements, since human and diabolical errors and lies are also accurately recorded.*

6. *The original New Testament was written in Aramaic and has been preserved to this day with 100% word accuracy in The 27 books of The Peshitta-Peshitto form I have tested, and in which I have found volumes of coded information.*

7. *Greek is not the original language in which any New Testament book was written.*

8. *The Greek New Testament is a translation of the original Aramaic text in all 27 books of the Western New Testament canon.*

9. *The number of letters in The original New Testament was and is 461,094. It is possible that the completed text as written approx. 1950 years ago had some few spelling differences in a few places or compound word division differences, but the total number of letters was the same.*

10. *God and His Son love you eternally, and have provided for your eternal welfare and joy.*

11. *Nothing can separate you from that love.*

I invite others to research this Aramaic text, as well as The Hebrew Old Testament, to see if the data supports or mitigates this position. More research is called for, especially with regard to The Hebrew Bible. I am confident that text will also yield data very similar to that found in The Peshitta, as already indicated in The Torah results (a probability of 1 in more than a thousand for an average ELS).

I have volumes of additional evidence confirming the above predictions. These are not codes, but computer word analyses which compare parallel word pairs in the respective Aramaic & Greek versions throughout The NT.For those interested in several additional studies and the raw data of my experiments, see http://aramaicnt.com .

Mt. 24:35 שמיא וארעא נעברון ומלי לא נעברן

Heaven and earth shall pass away, but my words shall not pass away.

- Marya Yeshua Meshikha
The LORD Jesus The Messiah